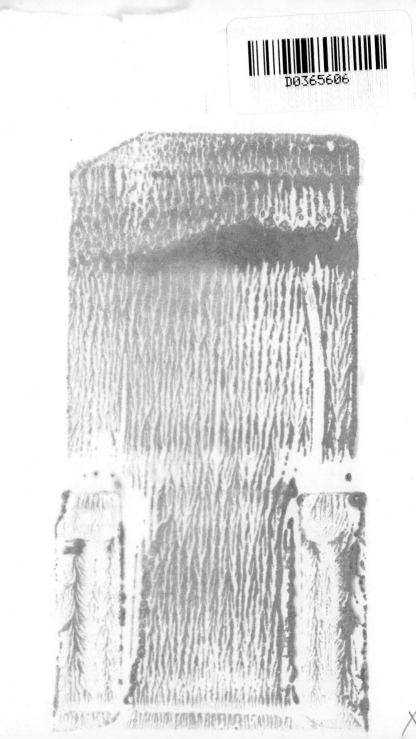

OUR
CHRISTIAN HOPE

GEORGIA
HARKNESS

OUR
CHRISTIAN HOPE

Abingdon Press
NEW YORK
NASHVILLE

OUR CHRISTIAN HOPE

Copyright © 1964 by Abingdon Press

Library of Congress Catalog Card Number: 64-19346

SET UP, PRINTED, AND BOUND BY THE
PARTHENON PRESS, AT NASHVILLE,
TENNESSEE, UNITED STATES OF AMERICA

DEDICATED TO

Harry Emerson Fosdick
Edgar Sheffield Brightman
Ernest Fremont Tittle

great servants of the Lord to whom I owe much

CONTENTS

INTRODUCTION

THERE ARE SEVERAL REASONS WHY THIS BOOK HAS BEEN written. The one which lies nearest the surface is the fact that there is too much superficial optimism and too little firmly grounded hope in the world today. Our society finds itself in the strange paradox of almost unlimited trust in the achievements and products of science, and at the same time of great mistrust of human nature and the possibilities of human happiness. One has only to pick up a newspaper or magazine, go to the movies, watch an evening's television programs, or read a contemporary novel such as William Golding's *Lord of the Flies* to find this paradox portrayed with startling clarity. Life is full of things to use and to enjoy, but human nature is full of evil impulses, and happiness seems to millions of persons an elusive dream.

A similar paradox is present in regard to the status of the Christian religion. In America the churches burgeon as to new buildings and programs and to a considerable degree also as to attendance and social acceptability. Yet there is much talk of this as a post-Christian era. Theological currents have drawn the gospel message closer to the Bible and to the faith of the Reformation than formerly, and this faith quite properly has less confidence in man's works, more in God's grace. Yet in the form in which it is commonly held and presented, it is open to question whether it seems more relevant to life, imparting a more lively hope to the millions who desperately need it. The paradox of our situation is evident in the fact that influential Christian voices alternate between deploring the inroads of secularism on biblical faith and seeking still further modifications of biblical faith to adapt it to modern thought.

This book has been written from the conviction that the ancient verities of our faith carry with them, for today as for every day, an abounding wellspring of hope. They must be restated from age to age. We cannot go back to the pre-Copernican, or pre-Newtonian, or pre-Darwinian, or pre-Einstein era. The God who has revealed himself supremely in Jesus Christ, the same yesterday, today, and forever, certainly does not expect us to go on using the same modes of communication forever. Yet the gospel message of divine goodness in the presence of evil, impelling us to faith amid despair, love in the face of man's inhumanity, hope in the midst of sin and pain and death, is a message that does not and cannot wear out.

My first reason, then, for writing this book is that I want to say in my own way, which need not be another's, what this word of hope is. If by God's grace it should stir some readers to fresh hope in the gospel message, this would be the best reward the book or its author could have.

Years ago I wrote a doctoral dissertation on "The Relations Between the Philosophy of Religion and Ethics in the Thought of Thomas Hill Green." It has never been published and never will be—nobody would want to plow through its 499 pages! I mention it only because, as I completed it under the direction of a beloved professor Dr. Edgar S. Brightman, I wanted to add a concluding chapter of "application to the present situation." With proper professorial acumen as to how a dissertation should be written, he advised me to "suppress my homiletico-pedagogical instinct." That, I believe, was the last writing I have done in which the instinct was suppressed! Furthermore, one does not serve as

professor of applied theology for twenty-two years without get-
ting the application habit, even were it not already ingrained.

A second reason for writing on this subject is the completion
of a series that was begun several years ago, designed to deal
with the major themes in the gamut of Christian theology. It
was not announced as a series, for I did not wish to be under
the pressure of expectancy to produce the next volume in it.
The books have not come out in the usual sequence of topics,
but as I felt impelled to write them. They have included books
on the foundations of Christian knowledge, God and his providence, prayer and the Christian life, the church, and Christian
ethics. I have not dealt specifically with salvation or Christology
for these themes have been incorporated throughout. The present volume aims to bring together the main things I believe on
the Christian doctrines of man, history, and eschatology.

The reader will find occasional references to these earlier
books, not because I wish to laud them, for there are numerous
better books available on all these themes, but for the practical
reason that there is no point in simply saying over what I have
said elsewhere at greater length. I have tried to say enough here
to give the principal substance of my thought, but the reader
will at various points find more of it in these other books if
he cares to pursue the matter.

Since reviewers have a way of labeling me sometimes as an
old-time liberal, sometimes as a neo-liberal, sometimes as a conservative (I have even been called, though not often, a Bar-
thian!), it may save them some trouble if I say that I have long
considered myself an evangelical liberal, and still do. The kind
of liberalism that has been castigated throughout the century
by the fundamentalists, and since the 1930's by the neo-orthodox,
I do not recognize as a true picture of the liberalism of those

who did most to mold my thought. Nor do I recognize it as the theology I have tried to teach, write, and live by. The affixing of labels is not the most useful theological occupation, but where they are used they should be accurate. As I shall later suggest in regard to particular topics, some theologians who chastise the liberalism of their fathers tend in doing so to whip not only a theological parent but a straw man.

There is a third interest that has prompted some aspects of this book, though not by specific reference until Chapter V. When the Third Assembly of the World Council of Churches was held at Evanston in 1954, its main theme was "Jesus Christ—the Hope of the World." After three years of deliberation by an advisory commission of top-ranking theologians of the world, and much general discussion of the first and second reports, a document was produced which is definitive for this theme as far as any such document can be said to be. It is no longer widely studied—in fact, the third and most satisfactory form of the report never was. For the past ten years I have wanted to say what I believe to be somewhat nearer the truth on the same subject, and this book is my opportunity.

For whom is this book intended? Mainly for ministers who are commissioned to proclaim the Christian hope and for laymen of some theological concern. It is hoped also that the theme, if not the treatment of it, will have enough vital interest to commend the reading of the book to some of the theologians. Since all Christians—ministers, laity, and theologians alike—must try to live by Christian hope, there is a sense in which it relates to all of us.

The more original sections of the book, and therefore probably of the greater interest to theologians, are to be found in the analyses of the various criteria of progress and their relevancy, various views of history, various kinds of myth, various doctrines of the kingdom, and the relations of immortality to resurrection. Too often, in my judgment, progress is abruptly dismissed, demythologizing is accepted or rejected, and the consummation of the kingdom whether on earth or beyond history is announced, without the drawing of clear distinctions as to terms. I do not claim to answer all the questions, but it may facilitate an answer to show the focus of the differences in competing positions. I think the reader will not be left in doubt as to where my own convictions lie.

I am not greatly worried as to whether readers will or will not agree with what is stated here, provided they have what seem to them firmer grounds of hope. This is my faith, and I must state it. I am somewhat concerned lest I seem not to enter sufficiently into the misery of the world's millions. It is true that "the lines have fallen for me in pleasant places," and I have had friends and opportunities far beyond my deserving. Such troubles as I have had pale into insignificance before the Lord's blessings. Yet whether or not *I* can enter fully into the acute suffering or the dull hopelessness of the less fortunate, *God can*. This is what really matters.

God's word of hope spoken through Jesus Christ to our human plight is what this book is all about.

I

THE GREATNESS AND
THE WRETCHEDNESS OF MAN

IT WAS THE PHILOSOPHER-SCIENTIST BLAISE PASCAL IN
the seventeenth century who laid the groundwork for the title of
this chapter. In spite of the fragmentary way in which his
Thoughts were left—almost like a set of incidental notebook
jottings, certainly not with the continuity demanded of any author of today who would expect to get a hearing—Pascal has
been speaking to the past three centuries. No one has ever more
realistically detected or more forcefully stated the incongruities
in man's nature. Sublime in the capacity for thought and reason,
noble in his ends, yet petty and even "abject and vile" in the
achievement of these ends, man persists in his self-centeredness
when his gaze should be directed toward his Maker. And with
his self-centeredness, largely given over to a quest for diversions,
comes misery rather than happiness.

Many passages could be quoted from Pascal to indicate this
ambivalence of human nature. The following is perhaps as arresting as any:

What a chimera then is man! what a novelty! What a monster, what
a chaos, what a contradiction, what a prodigy! Judge of all things,
imbecile worm of the earth; depositary of truth, sink of uncertainty
and error; the pride and refuse of the universe! [1]

---

[1] Blaise Pascal, *Thoughts,* tr. W. F. Trotter (New York: E. P. Dutton &
Co., 1931), 434.

14

Pascal has much to say about man's revolt against God, with the shame and misery which follow from the attempt to live without God. It is perhaps for this reason that he is so often quoted by theologians of the present who emphasize the darker side of human existence. Though he extols the greatness of man's mind, he has less to say of the biblical affirmation that man was made in the divine image. To Christian faith it is this spiritual kinship with God, with the capacity for thought or reason derivative from it rather than primary, which is the true ground of man's greatness. Although there are those of both past and present who contend that this image was wholly lost by the Fall, it seems a truer judgment to say that sin and self-centeredness continually mar but never fully efface the marks of human greatness. If this is true, man is redeemable, and there is hope for man even in his wretchedness. This is basic to the position to be presented in the ensuing chapters.

The purpose of this chapter is to present what the author believes to be the primary notes in the biblical view of man. This is a precarious undertaking for two reasons: first, that there is no single, systematic, or even fully self-consistent presentation of man's nature in the Bible; and second, that the biblical writers were not psychologists in the modern sense, and could have been mistaken as to some aspects of man's nature which are now being affirmed on scientific grounds. Were they as far wrong on this score as in their cosmology of a three-story universe? If so, they can teach us little.

These are formidable pitfalls. Yet I believe they are by no means fatal, and again for two reasons that match the dangers. These are: first, that there *is* an overall and permeating assumption about man's nature in the Bible which is discernible amid the disparities; and second, that modern depth psychology and

the insights of the most discerning and clear-visioned psychiatrists corroborate this view to a remarkable degree.

The net result is a picture of the greatness and the wretchedness, or the grandeur and the misery, of the man of the biblical
world and the man of today. To this man, Christian faith offers
hope both of the conquest of his wretchedness and the illumination of his greatness.

This view will be presented under several ambivalent cate-
gories, for anything less would be untrue to reality. The cate-
gories themselves "come mixed," both in the Bible and in man
as a living person, but for the sake of convenience of discussion
we shall try to sift them out.

1. Man as supreme creation and responsible creator

The affirmation with which the Bible opens, and which is
presupposed throughout its entire scope, is that God alone is
the Maker of heaven and earth. There are two creation stories
in Genesis. The first, running from Gen. 1:1 through Gen. 2:4a
is relatively late writing, postexilic in origin. The second, from
Gen. 2:4b through the remainder of the chapter, is a much
earlier piece of writing and on the whole less majestic and meaningful. They agree in declaring the ultimacy of God as the
Creator. Man is his creature, with a delegated responsibility to
have dominion over the lower animals and the things of nature.

Yet man is God's supreme creation. The first creation story
makes the creation of man the final act, and hence the climax
of all created things; the second puts the forming of man from
the dust of the earth to become a living being prior to the
vegetation he was to eat and the garden he was to till. This discrepancy in sequence is generally overlooked by those literalists
who insist on a six-day creation and the verbal accuracy of these

accounts. It causes no trouble to those who recognize that these accounts are prescientific and pictorial rather than factually accurate descriptions of how creation took place, and who read them for their great spiritual overtones. Both accounts intend clearly to indicate man's primacy as the supreme act of divine creativity.

There is a tendency in recent theology to try to counteract man's overweening sense of his own importance by stressing his creatureliness, and with it his sin and weakness. A weak and sinful creature man certainly is. But this ought not to overshadow the biblical emphasis on the worth of man to God, not only as God's prime creation to which all nature is subordinate, but as the recipient of God's steadfast love. Weak, sinful, and rebellious as man might be—and *was*, and *is*—God never forsakes him or regards him as of little importance. Indeed, this divine concern for man is the Bible's primary theme.

In the Old Testament, man's supremacy over even the majestic handiwork of God in nature is stated in the familiar words of the Eighth Psalm, voicing both skepticism and faith:

> When I look at thy heavens, the work of thy fingers,
>   the moon and the stars which thou hast established;
> what is man that thou art mindful of him,
>   and the son of man that thou dost care for him?

> Yet thou hast made him little less than God,
>   and dost crown him with glory and honor.
> Thou hast given him dominion over the works of thy hands;
>   thou hast put all things under his feet,
> all sheep and oxen,
>   and also the beasts of the field,
> the birds of the air, and the fish of the sea,
>   whatever passes along the paths of the sea (vss. 3-8).

These words are obviously reminiscent of the Genesis injunction to "fill the earth and subdue it; and have dominion" (Gen. 1:28) over the rest of the created world. Thus, by a divine vocation to stewardship in the conquest of nature, man becomes a creator, commissioned to act responsibly at the call of God.

Even the injunction to toil which follows the story of the Fall and the loss of Eden suggests pictorially that man's intended work in the conquest of nature is a God-given form of creative activity. Such toil may be viewed as a curse, a necessity for survival as the fruit of sin, and so it was regarded by the author of this early story. But because it is a God-given task, it may also be viewed as a blessing. The ambivalent nature of such work is expressed imaginatively by a lovely picture in Sholem Asch's *Mary,* where the boy Jesus, whom the author calls by his Hebrew name of Yeshua, is represented as working with Joseph to cut wood in the forest for the carpenter shop:

> "Today we have fulfilled the commandment of eating bread in the sweat of our faces," Yeshua said, smiling.
> "The commandment?" asked Joseph, who had never known the word applied to the divine curse.
> "Yes, *abba;* whatever God ordained for man is a commandment for good and to be taken as a blessing."
> Joseph pondered a moment and replied with a sigh of relief: "You have prevailed, my son. I see it now. Each of God's words to man is a benediction, never a curse. There is great joy in the sweat of one's brow." [2]

In the New Testament not much is said of man's creativity in the conquest of nature. Yet it is everywhere assumed that God is the Creator and man his supreme creation. This is linked, at least

[2] Tr. Leo Steinberg (New York: G. P. Putnam's Sons, 1949), p. 272.

by implication and sometimes by explicit statement, with the conviction that this imparts to man great worth.

We do not find in the Bible the words so often glibly spoken a generation ago, the "intrinsic worth of personality." Yet if one will look at the New Testament seriously, and in particular at what is recorded of the words and deeds of Jesus in the Synoptic Gospels, it becomes evident that to God his supreme creation is supremely worthful. It appears in the Sermon on the Mount in the question, in reality a great declaration, about the care of the Father for birds of the air and the lilies of the field: "Are you not of more value than they?" (Matt. 6:26-30.) Again, of the care of the Father who marks the sparrow's falling, Jesus affirms, "Fear not, therefore; you are of more value than many sparrows" (Matt. 10:31). The word *value,* central to much current sociological discussion but shied away from in theology, does not appear often in the Bible, but we find it again in the comparison of the rescued sheep with the healed man: "Of how much more value is a man than a sheep!" (Matt. 12:12.)

Such passages, if they stood alone, might not be enough to build a doctrine upon. Yet the total ministry of Jesus speaks more eloquently than any particular words. Everything he did, even to his death on the cross, was in service to men at the call of the Father. Not because men are supremely worthful through any natural right or merit, but because the climax of God's creative act is also the climactic object of God's loving concern, Jesus lived and died for us. This great fact, if no other, ought to make us think highly of man—and of all men.

2. The divine image and its distortion

Closely linked with the doctrine of creation and, indeed, inseparable from it is the biblical metaphor which has become

central in Christian theology, the image of God. The term appears
rarely in the Bible, twice in the Old Testament (Gen. 1:26-27
and 9:6); twice in the New Testament, but there quite inci-
dentally (I Cor. 11:7 and Col. 3:10). The basic reference is the
one in Genesis:

So God created man in his own image, in the image of God he
created him; male and female he created them. And God blessed
them, and God said to them, "Be fruitful and multiply, and fill the
earth and subdue it; and have dominion over the fish of the sea and
over the birds of the air and over every living thing that moves upon
the earth" (Gen. 1:27-28).

These ancient words, in spite of their primitive, prescientific
setting, speak to us today of our stewardship. But what do they
tell us of our nature? Why should the image of God, so rarely
again mentioned in reference to man, have become so basic in
Christian thought through the centuries?

One reason lies in the long debate, not yet terminated, as to
what the fall of man recorded in the third chapter of Genesis did
to this image. Another is the fact that the New Testament speaks
of Christ as the image of the invisible God (II Cor. 4:4; Col.
1:15); and of salvation through Christ as conformity to the image
of God's Son (Rom. 8:29). Thus, both sin and salvation are
linked with this concept. Yet, again, the specific references are
few.

The major reason why the term has persisted is that it is so
appropriate. To speak of man as made in God's image suggests
at one stroke the greatness of man and the source of this greatness. The Bible does not spell out the metaphysical implications
of man's likeness to God in terms of his capacity for moral decision and responsible choice and his ability to love, to think, and

to create; yet it everywhere implies these capacities. And because man misuses these God-given and godlike capacities, preferring his own self-centered desires to God's will and his own thoughts to God's wiser and holier designs, man sins.

About the prevalence of human sin, the Bible is unequivocal. Sin is essentially a religious term. It goes deeper than infractions of prevailing moral standards; it presupposes God and man's deviation from what God requires of him. Man's everpresent sinfulness and God's yearning desire to save him from it are the recurrent and dominant themes of the Bible. There is no need to cite specific references to sin, for it appears on every page in one form or another. Yet, with equal consistency, the biblical teaching on sin is never separated from the promise of divine mercy and forgiveness. The God of the Old Testament, with all of the stress on God's righteousness, is still a "God merciful and gracious, slow to anger, and abounding in steadfast love and faithfulness" (Exod. 34:6); and the God of the New Testament is the "God and Father of the Lord Jesus" (II Cor. 11:31). Repentance, acceptance, reconciliation, transformation, empowerment to new life through God's mercy and grace are basic notes in the relation of the sinner to his God.

What, then, do we mean by the image of God and its distortion? Few if any scholars today believe literally that there was once a pair of absolutely sinless human beings on earth who through a single act of disobedience in a garden at a point in history precipitated the curse of sin on all their descendants. Yet this does not destroy the realism in the Genesis story of man's creation in God's image and the distortion of this image through the Fall. That man is both godlike in his God-given capacities, though always finite in contrast with God's infinity, and is at the same time persistently a sinner, is stark realism. In this fact both the greatness and the wretchedness of man are centered.

At this point lies also the primary focus of Christian hope. What man is in human dignity and worth *in spite of his sin,* and what God does for man in love *because of man's sin,* epitomize the Christian gospel.

3. Man as nature and spirit

Man "stands at the juncture of nature and spirit." So states Reinhold Niebuhr in his epoch-making *The Nature and Destiny of Man.*[3] From this juncture come both man's proneness to sin and those capacities of the higher life which set man apart from the subhuman animal world.

Yet what do these terms mean? Clearly, an important aspect of "nature" is man's body and its organic needs. Without function- ing vital organs and enough food, water, air, and sleep to keep the body operative, man as a living creature on earth does not exist. The primary reference of the term "nature" is to the body, but the word can also be stretched to include man's instinctive drives, conditionings, habit patterns, and other aspects of his historical existence amenable to scientific measurement.

It is man's spirit, as distinguished from the nature that he so largely shares with the animal world, that makes man a person. This is harder to define. Classical philosophers, including Pascal, have often found this distinguishing trait in man's reason. It seems truer to say that its primary mark is man's freedom of deci- sion and choice, from which is derived man's capacity to tran- scend his circumstances to find meaning in his existence, to seek values in response to ideals and goals, to act with moral re- sponsibility, and in a religious sense to respond to God and seek

[3] (New York: Charles Scribner's Sons, 1941), I, 17.

to do the will of God. Such freedom of decision inevitably brings with it the power to sin.

It is man's spirit, not his body, that is made in the divine image. But what does the Bible say about this body-spirit relationship?

The Bible does not ordinarily make the sharp division between body and soul or the three-pronged division into body, mind, and spirit which have become embedded in both popular thought and the Christian tradition. The person, man (*adham* in the Hebrew, from whence comes Adam as generic man), is one person. The word *nephesh*, usually translated *soul* in the King James Version, means a living creature. In Gen. 2:7 the older rendering is: "And the Lord God formed man of the dust of the ground, and breathed into his nostrils the breath of life; and man became a living soul." The Revised Standard Version more accurately renders it "and man became a living being," and it is of some significance that the same word *nephesh* is used a few verses further on, in Gen. 2:19, for living creatures who from the context are obviously subhuman animals.

Yet this must not be taken to mean that the Bible supports a materialistic, much less a behavioristic, account of human personality. Man alone has those spiritual qualities that make him akin to God. The Bible takes for granted a unity of body and soul, but this does not make of man his body only. Where the writer feels the need to draw a distinction he does so; otherwise he treats the person as one living, morally responsible creature.

This tendency of the Bible writers to think of the person as one composite whole man was the natural outgrowth of a simple, prescientific, commonsense view. As you and I do not ordinarily stop to analyze the meaning of the "I" when we say, "I think this is so," or "I did wrong," or "I was sick," or "I got well," neither did the biblical writers. They were spared the need of analysis by the fact that the belief in personal existence after bodily death emerged late in Old Testament thought, coming into the foreground only in the intertestamental period, with the Pharisees, but not the Sadducees, believing in the resurrection. The persistence of this belief in the simple unity of the person is largely responsible for the fact that while the resurrection of Jesus is attested unequivocally by all four of the Gospel writers and throughout the rest of the New Testament, its nature is presented with far less consistency. As a result, the physical, though not wholly physical, imagery in which it is clothed makes its nature still a problem.

But we must note also that the unity of the whole person did not remain in biblical thought an undifferentiated unity. The contrast between body and soul appears more sharply in the New Testament than in the Old, but it is not wholly absent there. Though there is slight mention of the body by specific reference in the Old Testament, there are stipulations in Leviticus and Deuteronomy against the disfigurement of the body (Lev. 19:28; 21:5; Deut. 14:1), and there are the usual taboos of a primitive society against defilement through touching a corpse. The most important Old Testament passage on the body-soul relation is, unfortunately, one of which the text is uncertain. The Revised Standard Version renders the postexilic affirmation in Job 19:25-26 thus:

> For I know that my Redeemer lives,
>   and at last he will stand upon the earth;
> and after my skin has been thus destroyed,
>   then without my flesh I shall see God.

"Without my flesh" may also be rendered "in my flesh," with marked differences in the meaning.

However, it is in the New Testament that both the importance of the body and the supremacy of soul over body become most clearly drawn. Paul is emphatic as to the need to keep the body in subordination to the soul. What he says explicitly in I Cor. 9:27, "I pommel my body and subdue it, lest after preaching to others I myself should be disqualified," is implied repeatedly. In affirmative terms, this appears movingly in what is probably Paul's last letter, written from physically constricting circumstances in a Roman dungeon:

Not that I complain of want; for I have learned, in whatever state I am, to be content. I know how to be abased, and I know how to abound; in any and all circumstances I have learned the secret of facing plenty and hunger, abundance and want. I can do all things in him who strengthens me (Phil. 4:11-13).

Paul carries this need to subordinate the body to such lengths that he often uses the term *flesh*, not explicitly for sexual temptation or other enticements of the body, but for any evil impulse like jealousy or enmity which entices the sinner away from purity of life in obedience to God. A glance at what Paul regards as the "works of the flesh" as these are stated in Gal. 5:19-21, in contrast with the "fruit of the Spirit" in the verses which follow, makes evident this contrast in Paul's thought.

Yet Paul did not think of the body as wholly evil. No greater tribute could be paid to it than that which he gives in I Cor. 6:15, 19-20, where in protest against sexual immorality he exclaims:

Do you not know that your bodies are members of Christ? Shall I therefore take the members of Christ and make them members of a prostitute? Never! . . . Do you not know that your body is a temple of the Holy Spirit within you, which you have from God? You are not your own; you were bought with a price. So glorify God in your body.

Furthermore, Paul would hardly have spoken of the church as "the body of Christ," in a figure of speech which is still widely used to designate its interrelated unity (Rom. 12:4-5; I Cor. 12:12-27; Eph. 4:11-16), had he thought of the body mainly in terms of contempt.

Since Paul's letters are the earliest part of the New Testament, it has been appropriate to speak of them first. Yet the attitude of Jesus must be the more definitive. He says less about the body in what we have recorded of his sayings than does Paul. But there is a marvelous affirmation, which has many times given comfort and hope in the midst of bodily persecution, in the words: "And do not fear those who kill the body but cannot kill the soul; rather fear him who can destroy both soul and body in hell" (Matt. 10:28). Or, as the same passage reads in the Lucan version, but with an added turn of meaning: "I tell you, my friends, do not fear those who kill the body, and after that have no more that they can do" (Luke 12:4).

Beyond these words lies the fact that apparently Jesus never thought meanly of the body or of its needs. Food and drink and clothing, he says, are not man's highest needs, and in view of the Father's care they ought not to be sources of anxiety. Nevertheless, they are valid concerns. "Your heavenly Father knows that you need them all." (Matt. 6:32.) Wherever Jesus went in his ministry, he healed the bodies with the souls of men, defying prejudice and established religious practice to heal on the sabbath when human need required. This dual but related ministry to soul and body comes into particularly vivid conjunction in the healing of the paralytic when Jesus said to his inquisitors:

Why do you question thus in your hearts? Which is easier, to say to the paralytic, "Your sins are forgiven," or to say, "Rise, take up your pallet and walk"? But that you may know that the Son of man has authority on earth to forgive sins—he said to the paralytic—"I say to you, rise, take up your pallet and go home" (Mark 2:8-11).

The Bible, then, gives no clear delineation of the nature of the soul or of its relation to a physical foundation in the body. Yet there was a great certainty that man had been made by God for obedience to God, and there are strong intimations in the New Testament that such obedience requires the supremacy of spirit over bodily impulses and desires. This, with a vivid awareness of man's proneness to sin, was all the psychology that was known to the biblical writers or felt to be needed by them.

What is the bearing of this on man's situation in today's world, and in particular, on Christian hope?

There is an obvious bearing on the question of the continuance of personal existence after the death of the body, and of this we shall say more presently. Yet it is of great importance also to life in the present. A naturalistic description of the human ego, which makes the body and its functioning all there is of man, and which views man's choices and decisions as the deterministic result of his heredity and the conditioning of his neural mechanisms, is shaky ground on which to build morality, meaningful living, or religion. The popularization of this view is in no small degree responsible for the instability and loss of a sense of meaning which characterizes current society.

On the contrary, such a psychiatry as Viktor Frankl's "logo-therapy," or therapy through meaning, builds on the reality of human freedom, the will to meaning as basic to human existence, and the possibility of finding meaning in any human condition, however painful, horrible, and evil. To read his description of life amid the physical and mental tortures of Nazi concentration camps, yet with the preservation of human dignity through the spirit's transcendence of its circumstances, is to see vividly both the depths of human brutality to which man can descend and the heights to which the human spirit can rise when endued with a sense of meaning. His *From Death-Camp to Existentialism,* now revised and enlarged as *Man's Search for Meaning: An Introduction to Logotherapy,*[4] is a decisive answer to any naturalistic or deterministic interpretation of human behavior. Though Dr. Frankl's own background is Jewish rather than Christian, his psychological insights converge with Christian faith. On such a foundation, life can be strong and hope can be built.

4. Suffering and its transcendence

Sin is the deepest and most persistent element in man's wretchedness. Yet suffering is almost as omnipresent. Furthermore, it is far more commonly recognized as evil. Nobody but the masochist or the self-conscious martyr likes to suffer, and suffering is commonly protested against with defiance rather than accepted and transcended. It is the primary ostensible obstacle to Christian hope, and to all other forms of hope in human existence.

As is the case with the nature-spirit relationship, the Bible gives no systematic, clear-cut analysis of the source of suffering in God's good world. In short, it contains no theodicy by which to justify theoretically the ways of God to man in the presence of human pain. That sin brings about suffering through divine judgment is a dominant note throughout the Bible. This was often transposed, particularly in the Old Testament, to mean that

[4] (Boston: Beacon Press, 1962.)

the explanation of any suffering is to be found in sin, whether
overt or hidden from human eyes. The book of Job was written to disprove this popular assumption. This it does with dramatic power, though without presenting any real theodicy in
the words which the voice of God speaks from the whirlwind.
(Job 38:1–41:34.) The picture is of God's omnipotence, before
which Job must say, "I lay my hand on my mouth" (Job 40:4).

In the New Testament it is never questioned that sin justly
entails punishment. Yet that suffering must always be caused by
sin is an assumption explicitly rejected in words recorded as
spoken by Jesus. In Luke's Gospel it is stated that when word
was brought of Pilate's mingling the blood of the Galileans with
their sacrifices, he answered, "Do you think that these Galileans
were worse sinners than all the other Galileans, because they
suffered thus? I tell you, No; but unless you repent you will all
likewise perish." He continues with the affirmation that the eigh-
teen on whom the tower of Siloam fell were no worse than all
the other inhabitants of Jerusalem. (Luke 13:1-5.) Again in the
Gospel of John, Jesus refutes the idea that a blind man must
have incurred his affliction either through his own sin or his
parents' with the answer, "It was not that this man sinned,
or his parents, but that the works of God might be made manifest in him" (John 9:1-3).

Such passages help us to keep the sequence straight at two
vital points. First, sin *does* cause suffering, not always immediately but in its subtle and often in its overt effects. This is as true
today as when Paul wrote, "Whatsoever a man soweth, that
shall he also reap" (Gal. 6:7, KJV), and "the wages of sin is
death" (Rom. 6:23). Furthermore, the sin of an individual or a
group can drag many besides the sinner into its painful consequences, and this was never more evident than today as we

face the possibility of global destruction through man's sin and folly.

A second deduction is that we ought to be wary of supposing that *all* suffering is thus caused. Both uncharitable judgment of others and self-excoriation when tragedy strikes as the result of natural causes that could not be foreseen and prevented had best be put aside, and energy given to a constructive facing forward.

It is not my purpose here to try to state a theodicy. This I have tried to do as far as my limited wisdom will permit in an earlier book, *The Providence of God.*[5] What is important from the standpoint of Christian hope is not to understand why suffering comes, save as knowledge of its causes is an aid to its elimination. What is vital is to know that God is ever with us in the dark valleys of our pain, and that in the presence and power of God no pain is meaningless. Furthermore, if it has meaning for the enrichment of life, the enlargement of human sympathies, and a "closer walk with God," no pain is unendurable. The real climax of the book of Job is found not in his silence and sense of littleness before the Almighty, but in the words, "I had heard of thee by the hearing of the ear, but now my eye sees thee" (Job 42:5).

This message the Bible sounds again and again. Among the passages which spring immediately to mind are these:

The Lord bless you and keep you . . . and give you peace. (Num. 6:24, 26.)

In peace I will both lie down and sleep;
  for thou alone, O Lord, makest me dwell in safety. (Ps. 4:8.)

[5] (Nashville: Abingdon Press, 1960.)

Lord, thou hast been our dwelling place in all generations. . . .
Let the favor of the Lord our God be upon us,
    and establish thou the work of our hands upon us,
    yea, the work of our hands establish thou it. (Ps. 90:1, 17.)

Peace I leave with you; my peace I give to you; not as the world
gives do I give to you. Let not your hearts be troubled, neither let
them be afraid. (John 14:27.)

In the world you have tribulation; but be of good cheer, I have
overcome the world. (John 16:33.)

These are a few of the great promises of the Bible, not of
deliverance from pain, but of mastery of it by the power and the
presence of God. One less often quoted, but which goes to the
depths of the Judeo-Christian faith in its joy even within depriva-
tion and adversity, stands at the end of the book of Habakkuk:

> Though the fig tree do not blossom,
>   nor fruit be on the vines,
> the produce of the olive fail
>   and the fields yield no food,
> the flock be cut off from the fold
>   and there be no herd in the stalls,
> yet I will rejoice in the Lord,
>   I will joy in the God of my salvation (Hab. 3:17-18).

The current moods in art, poetry, philosophy, psychology, and
psychotherapy have much to say—often in symbolic terms—of
man's anxiety before the precariousness of human existence. This
is no new theme; the biblical writers knew it well though they
used other terminology. Yet not wholly other. Roger Hazelton
has aptly commented, "It comes with something of a surprise to
discover that the Bible employs similar tokens of anxiety—the

desolate pit, the miry bog, the flying arrow, the deep waters, the shadowed valley, and many others." [6]

Current solutions, though with variations, take one or the other of two courses. One is to assume that man ought to be happy as a natural right, and that in the thwarting of his hedonistic quest he must struggle to have his way even if entrenched moral standards are trampled in the process. The other is rooted in the assumption that the attainment of meaning through constructive service and love so far outweighs happiness that the latter need not much be thought about, though it comes as a by-product when higher goals are sought. There is no question that it is the second, whether it is called logotherapy or simply the peace of God, for which the Bible stands.

5. Man's last enemy

"The last enemy to be destroyed," says Paul, "is death" (I Cor. 15:26). This he speaks in an eschatological setting with regard to Christ's final triumph over the powers of evil. Yet with a more direct reference to our existential situation, these words are applicable to the human predicament. All men must die—there is no avoidance of this stark fact.

Whether through a biological impulse to survival which man shares with the animal world or through what is more significant, an implicit and usually unanalyzed recognition on the human plane that life is good, most persons want to live. This is not always the case. Suicide is evidence to the contrary, and it is not unusual in incurable disease or the ravages of old age to desire deliverance by death. Yet in normal circumstances and in the normal possession of one's powers, death is shunned, and it is delayed as long as possible.

[6] *God's Way with Man* (Nashville: Abingdon Press, 1956), p. 25.

The Bible takes this fact for granted, and nowhere tries to glamorize death. And in the earlier writings of the Old Testament, there is no attempt to question its finality. Even in the ambiguous passage from Job which may be translated "without my flesh I shall see God" (19:26), the overtones of the rest of the chapter are those of despair. There is a note of finality about death—which is startling to one accustomed to thinking in terms of the Christian hope—in Ecclesiastes:

For the fate of the sons of men and the fate of beasts is the same; as one dies, so dies the other. They all have the same breath, and man has no advantage over the beasts; for all is vanity. All go to one place; all are from the dust, and all turn to dust again (Eccl. 3:19-20).

Yet this passage, more likely to receive acceptance in an age of naturalistic psychology than in previous epochs of the Christian era, is not the Bible's last word. Gradually the conviction of man's immortality—or resurrection, as it was more commonly conceived to be—came into the ascendancy. Christ's own resurrection sealed this conviction, though it did not initially produce it. One has but to compare the words quoted from Ecclesiastes with those of Paul in the fifteenth chapter of First Corinthians to note the difference:

For this perishable nature must put on the imperishable, and this mortal nature must put on immortality. When the perishable puts on the imperishable, and the mortal puts on immortality, then shall come to pass the saying that is written:
"Death is swallowed up in victory."
"O death where is thy victory?
O death, where is thy sting?" (I Cor. 15:53-55.)

Current theology leans toward resurrection rather than immortality to avoid Platonic overtones of a natural immortality of the soul and to stress that eternal life is bestowed by God rather than something for man to claim in his own right. It also seeks to avoid the dilemma of a dualism in the soul-body relation whereby the body dies and the soul lives on. However, it is a transfigured body—not the corpse that goes into the grave or the crematorium—that lives beyond death by God's grace and power. This being the case, it has never seemed to me essential to draw the sharp line which some do between personal immortality and resurrection. Perhaps the term "eternal life" had best be used, for it covers both. We shall come to this again in Chapter VI.

In any case, it is the Christian faith that man is intended by God for a higher destiny, for he is not "like the beasts that perish" (Ps. 49:20). In this destiny, to be sought on earth and consummated in God's eternal kingdom, is the ultimate Christian hope. In this destiny, man's wretchedness is swallowed up in greatness even as death is swallowed up in victory.

II

THE STATUS

OF MODERN MAN

IN THE PREVIOUS CHAPTER WE TRACED THE OUTLINES of the biblical understanding of man, with only enough reference to the contemporary scene to give some evidence that the biblical view is not something far away and long ago but very relevant to the life of man in every age, including our own. The reason for beginning thus is that this is a book on *Christian* hope, and Christian hope is grounded in the revelation of God that is pre-eminent in Jesus Christ, but recorded for us in the Bible. Biblical theology is not the only valid type; we can learn of both God and man through nature, history, and human experience. Yet biblical theology is basic to any other.

In this chapter we shall shift the focus to the contemporary scene, and attempt to do three things. The first section will look at the paradoxes and dilemmas of modern man, in which his greatness and his wretchedness are mingled with startling vividness. This will be brief, for they have been traced many times in books and magazine articles, both secular and religious. This section is included both as illustrative of what was said in the previous chapter and as a stance for going forward.

The second section will survey the theological swings of the pendulum in regard to man over the past generation or, let us say, from the 1920's. The object of this survey is epitomized in the words cut in marble over the entrance of the Hall of Archives in Washington, D.C.—"The past is prologue."

The third section will take up three of the themes of the previous chapter. These are man's most ancient and persistent enemies, sin and pain and death. It is on these rocks that man's hopes are most often shattered. This is true in every age, including our own. Yet it is exactly at these points that Christian faith speaks its most vital words of Christian hope. If they are not spoken at these points with assurance and clarity by the exponents of religion, no one is going to listen much to whatever else may be said.

1. The paradoxes of modern man

To cite the now classic term of Dietrich Bonhoeffer, modern man has "come of age." He has a high degree of intellectual maturity, especially at the point of scientific knowledge, and no superstitions or myths purporting to be history will satisfy him. His sons and daughters go to college by the millions, and a college degree, essential for entrance into most of the skilled professions, is no longer the rare achievement that it once was. It has become an expensive commonplace.

In short, modern man knows a great deal—more, to be sure, in his own field of specialization than in broad general knowledge, but enough to make it appropriate to speak of intellectual maturity. Yet in many respects his outlook is parochial and limited. In two of man's most essential concerns, politics and religion, he is apt to be either a tradition-bound conservative or an iconoclastic liberal. In either case he tends to be swayed more by emotion than by wisdom.

A similar paradox prevails in his group achievements. On the one hand, there are scientific achievements in the nuclear space age that exceed the most fantastic imaginings of an earlier day. One does not need to be a very old person to recall his first glimpse of television, his first radio, his first sight of an airplane, perhaps even his first ride in an automobile. These are now utterly commonplace, and earth-encircling, man-made satellites startle nobody. Yet with these vast achievements of man's genius, man lives under a reign of terror that no previous generation ever knew. A slight miscalculation, a carrying of threats of force a step too far, and most if not all of the human race would be in the shambles of nuclear destruction.

Man's freedoms, whether political or personal, are also in curious disparity. To speak briefly of the former, every American ought not only to be proud of, but to thank God for, the degree of "liberty and justice for all" that may be exercised here in contrast with the restrictions that prevail in communist-dominated lands. Still, the mention of liberty and justice for all is a somewhat ironic reminder of the degree to which these are limited in our land. When basic human rights in voting, housing, employment, education, and the common amenities of life in a free society, including free access to churches, are denied to millions of American citizens because of their race and color, no American should take it for granted that this is a free country.

In the area of personal freedoms the evidence is equally paradoxical. In business, individual initiative is highly praised; yet it is conformity to prevailing economic practices that reaps the chief rewards. Education is theoretically person-centered; yet crowded classrooms and mass education make conformity the order of the day.

Such professions of freedom in conjunction with the actualities of conformity extend throughout our social life. Among both parents and their teen-age juveniles (whether or not delinquents) there are persistent demands for freedom from earlier social and moral restraints. However, group pressures to conformity were never more powerful. The freedom thus exercised seems to bring chronic discontent.

This is no new phenomenon. The desire to have one's own way and at the same time to be approved and admired by one's peers is as old as humanity. Yet it has taken new forms in the period which began in the 1920's. At the end of that decade Walter Lippmann described it graphically in a much-read book of that period, *A Preface to Morals*. Since the reader may wish to compare the situation of today I shall quote an excerpt from it:

> The evidences of these greater difficulties lie all about us: in the brave and brilliant atheists who have defied the Methodist God, and have become very nervous; in the women who have emancipated themselves from the tryanny of fathers, husbands, and homes, and with the intermittent but expensive help of a psychoanalyst, are now enduring liberty as interior decorators; in the young men and women who are world-weary at twenty-two; in the multitudes who drug themselves with pleasure; . . . in the millions, at last free to think without fear of priest or policeman, who have made the moving pictures and the popular newspapers what they are.
>
> These are the prisoners who have been released. They ought to be very happy. They ought to be serene and composed. They are free to make their own lives. There are no conventions, no tabus, no gods, priests, princes, fathers, or revelations which they must accept. Yet the result is not so good as they thought it would be. The prison door is wide open. They swagger out into trackless space under a blinding sun. They find it nerve-wracking.[1]

It is what the modern age has done to the human spirit that primarily prompts the writing of this book on Christian hope. I do not by any means think that the social situation is wholly bad,

[1] (New York: The Macmillan Company, 1929), p. 6.

or that man's plight is hopeless. In the next chapter I plan to cite some evidences that progress has taken place, not only over the entire sweep of human history but in the contemporary world. Yet the situation today is serious.

The man or the woman of today has a variety of sources of satisfaction—cultural, artistic, recreational, educational, even religious—unknown to the less colorful atmosphere of an earlier day. The general level of income in America, and thus the possibility of the possession of not only comforts but luxuries, is higher than ever before. People are living longer through marvelous advances in medical science, and there is no lack of interesting things to do in one's leisure time at any age.

Yet anxiety, rather than happiness, is the prevailing mood of our times. Part of it is due to the shadow of possible nuclear destruction and the uncertainties of the future, though to most persons their own immediate problems loom larger than the precariousness of the world situation. Part of it can be traced to the tensions produced by economic insecurity as automation increases and competition grows sharper—tensions which neither tranquilizing drugs nor the incessant smoking of cigarettes and drinking of black coffee in the offices will alleviate. Both at home and at work, irritability that mounts into suspicion and hostility readily bursts forth. The increasing prevalence of broken homes, drinking, and sexual irregularities is both cause and effect of the current social situation.

The prevalent anxiety cannot all be charged to social conditions. It stems primarily from a loss of inner meaning. Paul Tillich thus describes it:

The abyss of separation [from the Ground of our being] is not always visible. But it has become more visible to our generation than to the preceding generations, because of our feeling of meaninglessness, emptiness, doubt, and cynicism—all expressions of despair, of our separation from the roots and the meaning of our life. Sin in its most profound sense, sin as despair, abounds amongst us.[2]

2. Theological currents

In view of these facts it is not surprising that within recent years the psalmist's question, "What is man?" has swung into a place of centrality in both theological and popular thought. A generation ago the existence and nature of God and God's relation, if any, to an indifferent universe conceived in naturalistic terms, were at the focus of attention. Now it is mainly man, not God, that is the dominant concern of inquiring minds.

A possible exception to the last statement may be suggested by the fact that the most controversial theological book of 1963, John A. T. Robinson's *Honest to God*,[3] deals primarily with God. But does it? Both Robinson's approach and the writings of Tillich, whom he quotes extensively, are centered in the need to present an understanding of God which speaks to man's condition. One may or may not agree with their idea of God—I agree only partially—but one can scarcely doubt their understanding of and concern for the human predicament.

But let us take a brief backward look. Most of the naturalism of the 1920's and the years immediately before and after was avowedly atheistic, and the teacher of religion on a college campus had to reckon with its effect on student thinking, standards of value, and attitudes as these were influenced by the naturalistic assumptions of other departments. Naturalism was the more attractive in its appeal because it not only appeared to be scientifically grounded but, in conjunction with the preva-

[2] *The Shaking of the Foundations* (New York: Charles Scribner's Sons, 1948), p. 160.
[3] (London: SCM Press; Philadelphia: Westminster Press, 1963.)

lent humanism, it issued the call for more active and intelligent
social adjustment, the elimination of evil through knowledge and
goodwill, and the extension of human values.

John Dewey was the chief prophet of this movement, but he
had many understudies, and humanism, either as accepted or as
resisted, was a dominant interest of many persons both in and
out of the churches. Its most brilliant literary exponent, at least
among the philosophers, was Bertrand Russell, and his bravely
beautiful affirmation of unfaith in the famous essay, "A Free
Man's Worship," was widely quoted. Lest some readers have
forgotten it, or are too young to have heard it, a quotation may
suffice to indicate its spirit and that of a large segment of the
intellectuals of those years:

That man is the product of causes which had no prevision of the
end they were achieving; that his origin, his growth, his hopes and
fears, his loves and his beliefs, are but the outcome of accidental col-
locations of atoms; that no fire, no heroism, no intensity of thought
and feeling, can preserve an individual life beyond the grave; that
all the labours of the ages, all the devotion, all the inspiration, all
the noonday brightness of human genius, are destined to extinction
in the vast death of the solar system and that the whole temple of
Man's achievement must inevitably be buried beneath the debris of a
universe in ruins—all these things, if not quite beyond dispute, are yet
so nearly certain, that no philosophy which rejects them can hope to
stand.[4]

And this was written years before the appearance of nuclear fission brought a new threat of annihilation to mankind!

The prevalent religious liberalism of those years refuted this
position by showing that the laws of nature are the laws of God,
and hence there can be no real conflict between science and re-

[4] *Mysticism and Logic* (London: Allen & Unwin, 1918), pp. 47-48.

ligion. Fundamentalism, shocked both by this atheistic, humanistic naturalism and by the "modernism" often identified with it, retreated to its own literalistic interpretations of the Bible and talked about "science falsely so-called."

Henry Nelson Wieman, hoping to form a bridge between empirical naturalism of the Dewey type and Christian faith, proposed a theistic naturalism in which God was to be conceived as a more than human, immanent world process of growth in meaning and value, a principle of integration and concretion always at work in the universe. While for the most part this solution was rejected by both the groups he had hoped to bring together, it received wide attention in religious circles and had more than a little acceptance on university campuses.

All of these movements survive, but in somewhat altered form and without being any longer the center of attention. Naturalism as an exclusive reliance on scientific knowledge and method is widely prevalent, but it is less inclined to discredit the reality and worth of the human spirit. Humanism is still with us, but it is less optimistic, more self-critical, more interested in the nature of human relations and less in the rejection of theology, than it once was. Christian liberalism, often rejected and castigated by the new orthodoxy, survives, but in a more chastened, biblically grounded, and evangelical mood. There are still fundamentalists of all sorts, but its former leaders such as Edward J. Carnell and Carl Henry, editor of *Christianity Today*, represent a type of conservatism with more regard for biblical scholarship than in the past. The Wieman position has long been pushed into the background, but the recent publication of *The Empirical Theology of Henry Nelson Wieman*, a symposium edited by Robert W. Bretall in the Library of Living Theology series,[5] may revive it.

[5] (New York: The Macmillan Company, 1963.)

Not all the theistic issues are settled. There is an active concern as to whether Tillich's God as Being-in-itself—not *a* Being, but the unconditioned ground of all being—is really Christian, and existentialism, eschatology, and demythologizing are persistent current interests. Yet ever since the publication in 1941 and 1943 of Reinhold Niebuhr's two volumes of Gifford Lectures, *The Nature and Destiny of Man,* the Christian understanding of man has been dominant in theological thinking, and the differences between liberalism and neo-orthodoxy center at this point more than at any other.

It is easy to exaggerate the differences between these two schools of thought, for the differences lie much more in emphases than in positive affirmations or denials. As I have known no liberal theologian who would not freely admit the sinfulness and weakness of man, so I have known no neo-orthodox theologian who would deny that man was made in the image of God, God's supreme creation, and the object of God's infinite concern and yearning love. Still the impact through varying emphases has been noticeably different. The one approach has stressed the dignity of man—and of all men—as children of the one Father, and hence the obligation to honor, respect, and serve all men as brothers. The other approach has warned against human arrogance and self-righteousness, and has stressed the need and possibility of justification by faith alone. Both notes are needed; both afford a certain kind of Christian hope. But in the proclamation of its own deep convictions, each is prone to see error in the other. One reason, quite frankly, why this book is being written is that current trends in theology lay so large an emphasis on human sin and tragedy and on God's victory beyond history that too little attention is given to the grounds and possibilities of Christian hope within the earthly scene.

In popular circles also, the focus of inquiry has noticeably shifted from God to man. This is not to say that man has recently become more important than God, for Pascal was right that in every age men tend to think more of themselves than of their Maker. Yet if references in the press, especially the popular magazines, and in the theater, radio, and television may be taken as an index, people are less worried about God, more about themselves, than they were a generation ago. The resurgence of religious interest in America, however lacking in depth, has carried with it the tendency to regard belief in God once more as something intellectually respectable and not simply an outworn superstition —as something not very much understood but to be taken for granted. The matters of real concern are man's scientific achievements and whether the Russians are ahead of us in them, man's present prosperity and his threat of annihilation by nuclear power, the demands, both economic and social, constantly made upon the "organization man," his inner tensions, and his sources of satisfaction. Though salvation when it comes labeled in religious terminology can hardly be said to be a dominant popular interest today, modes of escape from boredom and insecurity, whether through free spending, surburban living, psychiatry, or religion, are much sought after and much written and talked about.

As a consequence we hear a good deal about man's "image" of himself as this is reflected in the essays, fiction, drama, poetry, music, painting, sculpture, and other forms of self-expression in our time. In general, such self-expression is marked by irregularity of form, eccentricity (which by its derivation means off-centeredness), syncopation, discord in the name of harmony. Traditional moral values and all other absolutes, if not rejected outright, are viewed with suspicion as relics of Puritanism and prudery. Religious values naturally fall under attack along with the rest, less through the conscious atheism of a generation ago than through an unconscious disregard of what the high religions have always stood for in the eliciting of religious devotion and reverence for the sacred.

Jazz has become the symbol of the age. Not only have attempts been made to express religious meaning in jazz forms, as in the putting of the Lord's Supper to jazz, but it has been seriously argued that since jazz expresses man's image of himself, while the ancient liturgies do not, the adoption of this medium by religious leaders is imperative.[6] To affirm the fullness of life in the modern age, it is said, we must abandon the outworn stereotypes and pious taboos of an earlier day for a medium that modern man understands because it reflects his characteristic moods.

Even if one does not go this far, it is scarcely arguable that the art reflects the culture of our time. Says another observer, who is competent in both the arts and in religion:

The truth is that it is not art that is sick, but society; the times are out of joint. In all periods of man's history art has reflected the fundamental character of the age, and it does so today. The paintings, the novels, the plays, the poems of the 20th century expose the disease of our civilization; man at war with himself, alienated from his fellows and his God, torn from the roots of his being.[7]

With the prevalence of such a mood, it is perhaps not strange that existentialism, both in its religious and antireligious forms, should have become popular in these days. Differing widely as they do, both the theistic and the atheistic brands of existentialism stress human experience and especially the human predicament

[6] Wilson Wade, "Jazz and the Image of Man," *The Christian Century*, November 29, 1961, p. 1424.

[7] Marvin P. Halverson, "If the Arts are to Return," *The Christian Century*, December 20, 1961, p. 1525.

of anxiety and loss of faith and hope until this is met by some answering element within the human situation. Not all forms of existentialism present such an answering element; for many of its exponents there is—to cite the title of Sartre's famous play— "no exit."

A minor warning to the reader may be entered at this point. I hope that this book may be in a true sense "existential," that is, grounded in the Christian revelation from God to man within the conditions of human existence. In a modest way I hope with Professor Tillich, though along a different path, to indicate how Christian faith answers the basic questions of man's existence. But my warning is that I shall not say much about existentialism. It is an ambiguous and often misleading term, standing both for brackish waters and sweet. When a word may be used of such disparate views as the atheistic nihilism of Jean-Paul Sartre and the varied Christian outlooks of Kiekegaard, Tillich, and Bultmann, it does not say much that is distinctive. Like its correlate, "realism," it can be used to praise or damn almost anything according to the point of view of the speaker. Yet in the sense that theology ought to deal with God's speaking to men within the conditions of their living—their hopes and aspirations, their joys and frustrations, their sinning and their sorrowing—it is profoundly important that this approach be kept uppermost.

3. Man's wretchedness—and Christian hope

Man's most ancient and persistent enemies, not by any means the products of our time but accented by its complexities and the overshadowing fear of nuclear destruction, are sin and pain and death. The fearful possibilities of the Cold War, the contrast between opulent and comfortable living and inner emptiness, the intensification of feverish activity and constant mobility, the tragic reminders which every holiday weekend gives of the transiency of human existence through death on the highways, these and many other aspects of our time bring home to us with fresh poignancy the reality of sin and pain and death.

We shall attempt in the remainder of this chapter to state what the Christian faith has been saying to man through many centuries in his confrontation with these perennial foes of the human spirit. This faith of ours, though very old, is by no means antiquated. It is as old as God's covenant with Israel, as Christ's ministry of compassion to human need, as his death and rising again for us. It is as contemporary as the guilt-ridden or depressed person's quest for psychiatric help, a mother torn with anxiety for her hopelessly sick child, the open grave of one who is loved but will not again be present with us on earth.

It is these ancient enemies that, with all man's greatness of mind and soul as he comes from the Creator, made in his image, induce man's wretchedness. So, what has our faith to say to them? [8]

Today we do not hear as much about sin as our fathers did. Many recoil from the word, and if they use it at all, think of it mainly as the grosser sins condemned by society—murder, adultery, drunkenness, overt lying, stealing, embezzling funds. And since, being respectable people, they do not do any of these things, they do not think of themselves as sinners—or at least as very bad sinners. Almost everybody will admit that he has a few faults and is not perfect. But most of us think we are as good as the next fellow, which being interpreted by a rationalizing conscience means "good enough."

It is to such moral dullness that the Christian gospel, when it

[8] Some paragraphs in what follows are restated with minor changes from Chapter XV, "The Christian Hope," in my *The Modern Rival of Christian Faith: An Analysis of Secularism* (Nashville: Abingdon Press, 1952.)

is really gospel and not merely a sermonful of conventional moral platitudes, speaks with the cutting force of a two-edged sword. It strips off our alibis, plunges through our respectable veneers, probes down to our selfishness so carefully concealed from ourselves and, we think, from others, and indicts us of self-centeredness even in our good works. It convicts us of pride, of envy, of anger, of jealousy, of pettiness, of compromise, of narrowness, of complacency before the agony of the world. The Christian gospel, when it has a human vehicle through which it can speak, confronts the supposedly well-off sinner of our day, who thinks there probably *are* sinners but they are somebody else, and says to him with terrible potency, "Thou art the man!"

We have been speaking as if the people of our time did not know they were sinners. Many do not. But again many do. Guilt is no outworn phenomenon. Relatively few in our society, I am inclined to think, think of themselves in the deeper religious sense as guilty before God. But hosts of people know they have done wrong. They have sinned against someone they love, or have betrayed a trust, or have let the lusts of the flesh overpower them, or in some other respect have failed to act with integrity and honor. And the result is a guilty conscience, a terribly torturing, soul-disrupting sense of moral failure. Every psychiatrist has to deal with folk whose fundamental problem is a moral one and who cannot be helped until this fact is clearly faced. Psychiatrists differ as to how best to get rid of a sense of guilt, but none doubts its reality or its deadly, disrupting, and corroding effects on human personality.

What then has the Christian gospel to say to either of these types of sinners, the moral sluggard who sees no sin in himself or the guilty neurotic whose guilt is tearing his life apart? Or to the rest of us, who lie in between and perhaps have some of both in us? The word of the Christian gospel is hope. It says not only, "You must be born again," but it assures us that we can. In a thousand ways the Bible assures us that he who turns to God in repentance, by faith, in commitment to God of our burdens as well as our virtues, and in earnest effort to bring forth fruits meet for repentance, God will in no wise turn away.

All of us, if we have a modicum of moral honesty, must say at times, "I do not do the good I want, but the evil I do not want is what I do." Some of us are impelled to say, in other words but with the same deep anguish of despair, "Wretched man that I am! who shall deliver me from the body of this death?" The answer in either case is Paul's answer, "I thank God through Jesus Christ our Lord. . . . There is therefore now no condemnation to them which are in Christ Jesus. . . . For the law of the Spirit of life in Christ Jesus hath made me free from the law of sin and of death" (Rom. 7:25–8:2, KJV). Here lies our fundamental Christian hope.

In the matter of pain we must speak with more reservations, for the Christian faith affords no hope that all pain will be blotted out of human existence. Nowhere in the gospel are Christians promised freedom from pain. "The whole creation," says Paul, "has been groaning in travail together until now" (Rom. 8:22), and this *now* of the first century is equally applicable in the twentieth. Furthermore, for the Christian who takes seriously the way of the Cross, reaching out to serve others in suffering love, his pain may be increased rather than diminished.

Nevertheless, says Paul also, "We are saved by hope" (Rom. 8:24, KJV). "In everything God works for good with those who love him." (Rom. 8:28.) Let us note that the translators of the Revised Standard Version of the Bible, without trying to secure a better theology but only a more accurate translation, have put much greater power and meaning into this statement than the older rendering, "All things work together for good to them that love God"—an affirmation which too often seemed repudiated by the facts.

Some differentiations are in order as to kinds of pain. Does Christian faith alleviate physical pain? Yes, sometimes and under some conditions. We may well believe that the God whose Son so often healed men's bodies in compassion and who has placed within our bodies so many regenerative elements to combat disease, desires for his children soundness of body as well as of mind and spirit. It is not irrelevant to pray for healing and, so far as this is possible within the order of God's world, to expect it. But to clamor for it, or to expect the laws of nature to be set aside for us, or to neglect the "means of grace" that good hygiene and medical science make available, is self-centered arrogance rather than good religion.

Every person of maturity knows that overt, tangible physical pain is not the hardest kind to endure. It is when insecurity, frustration, fear, tension, and inner conflict assail the spirits of men that our greatest testing comes. Many a person who has been able to meet a severe illness with only a minor amount of rebellion and complaint, so long as he believes it to be temporary, quails before the nagging, energy-sapping demands of daily living. Self-pity and rebellion intensify this mood, which to an alarming degree has become characteristic of our time.[9] In part, this aspect of man's wretchedness can be charged up to his self-centeredness. The best antidote, if one can muster the willpower for it, is to look beyond self in service to others. Yet this is not

[9] Note the evidence in the literary productions of this period cited by Robert E. Fitch in *The Odyssey of the Self-Centered Self* (New York: Harcourt, Brace and Company, 1961.)

THE STATUS OF MODERN MAN

a cure-all, for when one's fondest hopes are shattered and one has to adjust himself to the sudden and perhaps irrevocable loss of health, or financial security, or family ties, or loved ones removed by death, almost anybody finds the strain demanding of him more than he has.

Gripped by this kind of pain, which itself takes many forms but has a common center in a deep, inner unhappiness, how does the human spirit respond? Perhaps by a neurotic disturbance that sends one to the psychiatrist, or which prompts one lacking such professional help to tell his troubles to any who will listen. Perhaps by a deep inner loneliness that builds about one's ego a stony wall of silence. Perhaps—and this is one of the evidences of the true greatness of man—by stoic fortitude. Stoicism is never an adequate substitute for Christian faith, but when it comes from disciplined firmness of character that is able to take the storms of life, bowing before them without being broken, and carrying on in spite of them, it ought to be admired instead of being disparaged. A year spent in Japan, where such a disciplined endurance of pain is a welcome relief from the self-pity and comfort-seeking so common in the West, has intensified for me this respect for stoical self-control.

Yet with the strongest self-discipline, there are occasions when the hurt is so deep that it seems nothing will avail. Creative work to do, the comradeship of friends, the healing touch of time— all these help, for all these God has given us for our good. None of these is quite adequate, however. It is then that Christian faith and the knowledge of the love of God, if these have been made not a casual addendum but an integral part of one's being in smoother and more commonplace days, provide an impregnable bastion of hope.

"But what if I find no comfort in God?" the distressed soul is prone to say, thus echoing the poignant lament of Job, "Oh, that I knew where I might find him" (Job 23:3). It is true that nervous tension may itself set up a barrier that for a time hides God from sight, and not all failure to find God in time of need is due to shallowness of Christian experience. If the reader is interested, he will find that I have dealt with this at some length in an earlier book, *The Dark Night of the Soul*.[10] Nevertheless, whatever the vividness or the dimness of one's emotional awareness of God's sustaining hand, the Christian has grounds for knowing by faith that God is with us in the dark. To know this with the mind is not all we need, but it gives ground to stand on while firmer foundations are being built, just as it is also true that in theological doubt a vital emotional rootage gives stability. If we can believe, in the deeper springs of our being, that "in everything God works for good with those who love him," it is possible to face sickness, or deep disappointment, or separation from loved ones, or even death, and still say with Paul, "Who shall separate us from the love of Christ? Shall tribulation, or distress, or persecution, or famine, or nakedness, or peril, or sword? . . . No, in all these things we are more than conquerors through him who loved us" (Rom. 8:35, 37).

Yet neither sin nor pain is man's most intractable enemy. Says Paul again, "The last enemy to be destroyed is death" (I Cor. 15:26). The most irrevocable fact of life is death's inevitability, a fact which every man knows but which takes on a new urgency as he grows older and sees his friends, one by one, drop from sight. Though the modes of death's coming are infinitely variable —some easy, some terrible—there is no human way to make the death of a loved one seem good. It can be seen as the natural and necessary termination of the body's life, and in incurable or

[10] (Nashville: Abingdon Press, 1945.)

extremely painful illness as a benign release for which to thank God. Yet the grief remains. Even in the expected, and in a sense welcomed, death of an aged senile parent or friend or life partner, the pain of separation is inevitable.

Here, too, Christian faith redeems man's wretchedness with hope. That even the most secular-minded generally desire for their loved ones a funeral or memorial service at which the great assurances of religious faith are spoken is tacit recognition of the pervasiveness of this hope.

Yet this is not to say that all is as it should be in our society. Our abnormal and unchristian attitude toward death is one of the worst symptoms of a disordered culture. We sometimes smile with a sense of superiority at our forefathers' preoccupation with the other world. How could anybody, we say, ever think that the Christian's primary task is to fit his soul for heaven, or believe that life is a pilgrimage in which this life is but a brief interlude leading to eternity?

Certainly, too much preoccupation with heaven and hell can become morbid and escapist. If the vista of eternity is not connected with a sense of the sacredness of the present life, the emphasis is off-balance. Yet distortion appears also if the vista of eternity is omitted. Said John Wesley, "Our people die well." And they died well, as they lived, in the encompassing assurance of the presence of God, the transiency of this mortal scene, and the enduring reality of the larger life with God.

So perhaps it is we in our time who have become abnormal. We paint up the deceased to try to make him look "natural," which usually means very unnatural, for death has its own beauty; we have an expensive funeral, usually with many beautiful floral tributes; kind and gracious words are spoken; there are gestures of deference toward religious faith, for a minister, priest, or rabbi

conducts the service. Then it is over, and the bereaved must re-
build his or her life on such foundations as are left, wondering,
doubting, hoping that the separation is not permanent, but with
a great void there is no sure faith to fill.

Part of this is in the temper of the times. People do not like to
think about death until they have to, and when it is forced upon
them they stumble or flounder like a paralytic trying to walk
with unused muscles. Yet part of this uncertainty is also due to the
fact that the Christian understanding of death is so seldom
spoken about in the churches except at Easter services or at
funerals. Because the Christians of an earlier day centered too
much of their thought upon another world, we normally—and
abnormally—think too little about God's promise and the hope
of eternal life.

The result is that in the midst of a society with much to make
life rich and fine there is probably less joy than among those we
are prone to speak of as "joy-killing," otherworldly Puritans. In
a society that loves life, multitudes fear death. In a world in
which there is much to live for and manifold good causes to
which to give oneself, many flee from life by self-slaughter. Our
neurotic age cries out for a faith in eternity that would put meaning into time.

It is the Christian hope that to life lived in the presence of
God, death is but the entrance into a larger life. It is the Christian
hope that in the larger fellowship of God's sons for time and
eternity, there is no final separation from those we love. It is the
Christian hope that whether death comes early or late, no life
is fruitless, no personality prized by God as an infinitely precious
creation is snuffed out like a candle in the dark. It is the Christian
hope that even if new and more terrible weapons should destroy
all life upon this planet, God would not be ultimately defeated

or his kingdom destroyed. It is the Christian hope that Christ is the resurrection and the life, and that neither life nor death can separate us from the love of God which is in Christ Jesus our Lord.

In this faith millions in the past and many in our own time have lived and died victoriously. Thus is the wretchedness of man overcome, not by his own greatness, though this is real, but by the greatness of the love of God.

III

CAN WE
BELIEVE IN PROGRESS?

IN THE LATTER HALF OF THE NINETEENTH CENTURY, and roughly in the first third of the twentieth, there was a widespread belief in progress. This was grounded partly in the evolutionary optimism by which the scientific evidences for biological evolution were assumed to be somehow paralleled in the social scene, and partly in the empirical situation wherein things seemed to be moving along pretty well for the Western world. In religious circles, the doctrine of progress was also associated with the emphases of liberalism on the progressive revelation of God, the progressive coming of the kingdom of God on earth, and the social gospel by which man was called to assist in bringing this about.

The belief in progress was somewhat shaken by the First World War, but with the rapid recovery in the years that followed it continued to be held until the combination of the great depression, the rise of Nazism, and the coming of neo-orthodoxy converged to question its optimistic assumptions.

Today, the belief in progress is almost universally repudiated in theological discussion along with the liberalism that was associated with it. In secular liberalism, and the scientific humanism often linked with it, the standing of progress is tenuous and indecisive, but on the whole higher than among the theologians.

This chapter is included because I believe we ought neither

to be so blithely optimistic about progress as many were a generation ago nor so pessimistic about its possibility as is the mood of
our day. Properly understood in relation to foundations in biblical faith, it is a legitimate aspect of the Christian hope. Yet what
these foundations are, and indeed what progress is, require considerable probing. No casual statement that there has been
enough progress in human history so that we may hope for it in
the future will meet the situation.

1. Is there a pattern in events?

However, before we tackle a nest of problems in regard to
progress, a prior one must be considered. Is there any pattern at
all in human events? Or do they all "come mixed," just as they
happen to happen? If this is the case, no philosophy or theology
of history is possible except the denial of its possibility. All that
can then be done is to trace the sequence of events with their
precipitating causes, and abandon the search for trends or overall
movements, including the question of progress.

This is the view of some historians. George A. Buttrick in
Christ and History quotes both the statement of H. A. L. Fisher
to this effect and the comment of E. H. Carr that it is a "banal re-
mark":

Men wiser and more learned than I have discerned in history a
plot, a rhythm, a predetermined pattern. These harmonies are concealed from me. I can see only one emergency following upon another
as wave follows upon wave, only one great fact with respect to which,
since it is unique, there can be no generalizations.[1]

[1] (Nashville: Abingdon Press, 1963), p. 75. The quotation cited is from
the preface of H. A. L. Fisher's *A History of Europe* (Boston: Houghton
Mifflin Company, 1935); the ensuing comment is from E. H. Carr, *What Is
History?* (New York: Alfred A. Knopf, 1962), p. 52.

The truth, in my judgment, lies in between this somewhat iconoclastic dismissal of all patterns and the view that we can find a clear and unmistakable pattern into which all events can be fitted. But if either extreme must be qualified, how?

One often hears the aphorism, spoken as if it were certainty, "History repeats itself." There is some justification for this in the observed sequence of events, whether in the rise and fall of empires or in the outcropping of personal traits in a family. Yet it is also possible to deny completely the repetitive character of history when the emphasis is placed on the uniqueness of every situation. Both judgments are true from a particular perspective.

History is essentially a matter of human decisions and the consequences of these decisions. It is man who acts, not a set of automatic or mechanical physical forces. Man is endowed by his Creator with the freedom, always within limits, to choose his course and direct his own destiny. As he does so he affects the destinies of many others; yet these others also, however limited in their freedom, are always something more than robots. It is this power of free decision that constitutes the basic character of the human spirit. Whether emphasized as the power of moral decision, or of rational reflection, or of self-transcendence in the light of goals and ideals beyond immediate impulse, man's freedom sets him apart from every natural object or subhuman animal organism.

History can never be completely repeatable for this reason. No two persons are exactly alike, and as a consequence no two sets of circumstances can be identical. It is a commonplace fact that the home, community, or nation one is born into, varying in economic affluence, cultural advancement, moral and spiritual ideals, and much else, makes a great difference in one's adjustment to life. Yet even within what is relatively the same time and place and surrounding environment, the human equation provides for variability and makes exact prediction of human acts impossible. Not only is every human individual unique, but in the meshing together of lives in even the most conformist society no two circumstances are quite the same. Accordingly, whatever the general trends that may be evident, history never quite repeats itself.

This may be granted, and still the basic problem remains. Is there any "wave of the future" which can be counted on because of similar waves in the past? Is there something in the very nature of human beings, of physical nature, and of their conjunction in the events of history in which a pattern can be discerned? Hence, is the future relatively predictable? These questions are of great importance because they are closely bound in with the question of whether human existence has any meaning beyond a passing series of pains and pleasures.

The oldest of such concepts to be developed in the reflective thought of the Western world was the Greek idea of the *cyclical view of history*—of the sequence of events turning around like a great wheel, but without any forward movement and eventually coming back to the place of beginning. This was prompted by the observation of changes in nature and in the social and political world, giving rise to the longing for a foundation of permanence. Yet no permanence was found within history—only the certainty of change within the bonds of an inexorable Fate. The Greek gods were themselves subject to Fate; hence this view was essentially tragic and appears again and again in Greek tragedy.

This conception of a fixed but meaningless round of events appears also in full force in Epicurean philosophy, with its emphasis

on the enjoyment of fleeting pleasures because there is no hope
for the future. Toward the end of the Old Testament period this
had its impact on a nameless writer who calls himself Koheleth,
or the Preacher, and the book of Ecclesiastes rings the changes
on the unchanging character of existence with "Vanity of vanities!
All is vanity" as a dominant theme. "What has been is what will
be, and what has been done is what will be done; and there is
nothing new under the sun." (Eccl. 1:9.)

It is apparent that this sense of the futility of existence, though
without so much emphasis on coming to full circle in the round
of experience, is echoed in much of the existentialist drama,
poetry, and essays of our time.

The emergence of Hebrew-Christian thought gave a radically
new emphasis, which will be later dealt with at length [2] and is
therefore only briefly mentioned at this point. It is *linear and
forward-looking, rather than cyclical.* It centers in a God both beyond and within the currents of history, the Creator of the world
and all its people, to whom he gives loving concern in both judgment and redemption. Therefore, neither tragedy nor pleasure-
seeking can be ultimate notes in human existence, and existence
under God has meaning and hope.

It is neither a cyclical nor the Hebrew-Christian view of history that is chiefly emphasized today by social scientists, but
the discovery of *trends and characteristic behavior patterns
through a combination of natural with human causation.* We shall
for the present center attention here.

Human acts always take place within natural structures which
influence social history. A whimsical but realistic illustration is
Pascal's observation about the connection between the length

[2] See Chapter IV.

of Cleopatra's nose and the subsequent course of history.[3] However, the major determinants of human history by natural causes are to be found in economic and geographical factors that condition the course of backward and advanced cultures, and that affect the outlook of nations relatively secure up to the atomic age in contrast with those that have known war and conflict throughout most of their history.

History, we said earlier, is unrepeatable because of human freedom. Yet human nature has its characteristic tendencies. Among these is a great mixture of capacities for love, cooperation, and mutual concern with egoism, hostility, and the will to secure possessions, power, and prestige at any cost. These impulses are intensified by group loyalties and enmities.

From what we know of both natural and human causes of events, the course of history presents many lessons from which wisdom for the present and signposts—though never blueprints —for the future may be drawn. Some of these are so obvious that any unprejudiced observer can discern them. Among these are: (1) that strife breeds strife, while cooperation encourages cooperation; (2) that men prize freedom, but will surrender it for security; (3) that in times of insecurity, whether due to hunger, despotism, war, or the threat of war, moral restraints are easily cancelled; (4) that in any conflict the "in-group," that is, our side, always feels superior to the "out-group," and readily finds moral justification for its acts; (5) that in this self-justification of even the most heinous procedures, the blessing of deity is invoked, or in the unusual circumstances of an atheistic ideol-

---

[3] The quotation is, "Cleopatra's nose: had it been shorter, the whole aspect of the world would have been altered." *Thoughts*, 162. When quoted the adjective is often changed, perhaps more appropriately, to "longer."

ogy, the currents of history are viewed as giving assured victory to dialectical materialism.

Thus there is discernible a pattern in history which does not give full support to a doctrine of progress. In spite of temporary alleviations and now and then "the good years," history in large measure is the story of conflict, disharmony, and suffering. Yet this is not the whole story. As there has been dissension throughout the course of history, so have there been cooperation and mutual helpfulness. The darkness of conflict has never been able to quench the yearnings of some men for truth, beauty, and goodness, and of many persons for freedom, dignity, and self-respect. Civilization has gone forward in spite of great odds.

The trends of history are by no means all downward. There is evidence for believing that progress, though limited in scope, is a genuine aspect of human existence. But before we can make this statement with assurance, we must first ask what progress is. This requires the setting up of a criterion or, as we shall soon see, several criteria.

2. What constitutes progress?

A negative but commonly agreed upon approach to the meaning of progress is that it does not signify endless change—a succession of meaningless occurrences—but change in a direction believed to be more desirable. But believed by whom? And desirable for what? And made evident by what kind of factors? These are our questions.

Among the various criteria of progress four stand out with considerable clarity in distinction from one another, though with blurred lines at the edges. There is, first, advancement in man's conquest of nature through increased technical skills and increased production of desired material goods to enable man to live with greater ease and comfort. There is, second, the matter of advance in what is sometimes described as a "humane and civilized culture," with attention to the arts and the humanities, to the pursuit of knowledge, to gracious living, and to what in secular terms is often called "the good life." There is, third, greater social organization and the ability to live harmoniously in ever-widening units of social, political, and economic life. There is, in the fourth place, the question of advance in moral and spiritual values, with a deeper concern for God and neighbor and a greater willingness at personal cost to accept responsibility for the common good.

These criteria are not mutually exclusive. Each is important in its own context, though some are more important than others. As we look at each, we shall note what facts there are to substantiate the belief that, according to this criterion, progress has or has not taken place.

It is obviously the fourth of these types of progress which is in most dispute today, while serious questions are raised about the second and third. Only the first is unquestioned, and in view of the poverty, undernourishment, overpopulation, disease, and illiteracy of great segments of the earth's people, the affirmations made about advances in technical progress must be qualified by noting that these are as yet by no means universal.

Yet highly significant advances in *man's conquest of his material environment* there undoubtedly have been. These began, and were observed appreciatively but with skepticism as to their spiritual import, long before the emergence of modern science. Augustine, writing in *The City of God* in the first quarter of the fifth century, has this to say of the technical achievements of his day:

What wonderful, what stupendous results human industry has reached in clothing and housing! How it has advanced in agriculture and navigation! With what variety of invention it has thought out the designs of vases, statues and pictures, and with what skill executed these! What wonderful spectacles are exhibited in the theatres, incredible to those who only hear report of them! How many ways have been found of catching, killing and taming wild animals! For the destruction of men themselves how many kinds of poisons, weapons and mechanical contrivances have been discovered, and how many medicaments and appliances for the preservation and restoration of their health! What condiments have been found to stimulate the appetite and please the palate! And what a multitude and variety of signs there are to express and communicate our thoughts, with speech and writing as the chief among them! What graces of rhetoric there are to delight the mind! What a wealth and diversity of songs to soothe the ear! What musical instruments and styles of harmony have been devised! What expertness has been reached in measures and numbers and in tracing the orderly movements of the stars! None can exhaust the tale of what thought has thus discovered, especially if instead of such a general view details were to be mentioned.[4]

That was fifteen centuries ago! If Augustine from the Celestial City were to look upon today's world, he would observe astonishing developments. Yet doubtless his judgment would be unchanged. This was to the effect that, great as are the powers the Creator has endowed man with, these achievements provide no true and lasting felicity, and serve rather to accent the wickedness and misery into which man has fallen by the perversion of these powers.

This judgment is echoed by many today to point to the contrast between our spiritual shallowness and the wonders of

[4] I am indebted to *The Belief in Progress* by John Baillie (New York: Charles Scribner's Sons, 1951), p. 20 for the discovery of this remarkable passage, which he quotes at greater length than I have done here. It appears in *De civitate dei*, xxii, 24.

our technological achievement. That there is such a contrast is hardly debatable; it has become a truism. Yet the matter has another side. This is the genuineness of the benefits that have come to mankind through technological advance—benefits that we may well believe to be consistent with the will of God and that from the Christian obligation to love of neighbor ought to be shared as widely as possible with all men.

Lewis Mumford in his *Technics and Civilization*[5]—an excellent book even though now a fairly old one—traces the stages of technological development through the past ten centuries. The first period, extending from the tenth century to the middle of the eighteenth, is the period of wood and water as basic materials and sources of power. Among the life-changing inventions of this period were glass-making, facilitating indoor lighting, adorning great cathedrals, providing spectacles for defective eyes, making available the microscope and telescope; the perfecting of the clock as an instrument of precision, inaugurating a time-conscious age that has persisted to the present; the invention of the printing press with its vast possibilities for the dissemination of knowledge and the molding of opinion. The second period, dating from about 1750 and extending into the first half of the nineteenth century, was based mainly on coal and iron. During this time the steam engine came into its own, paving the way not only for the Industrial Revolution through great numbers of factories, but making possible a revolution in transportation through the railway and steamship. Then followed the age of electricity, interpenetrating but not replacing coal and iron as sources of power. With it came many new synthetic compounds, producing metals of greater lightness and compactness and a vast array of consumers' goods.

[5] (New York: Harcourt, Brace and Company, 1934.)

In this period emerged also a new concern for medical research, surgical cleanliness, and a widespread interest in sanitation which has done much to conquer disease. Since Mr. Mumford wrote, the field of electronics has added television to our equipment, bringing the events of the world into millions of living rooms, and atomic fission has not only opened up dread possibilities of destruction but potentially great new sources of power for peaceful uses.

This brief survey makes evident a commonplace fact—that with all the liabilities of the machine age in terms of over-anxiety for material goods, overstrain for their production and acquisition, and the unemployment that comes with displacement of human labor through automation, we would not retreat from technology if we could. I know of no one whose mind yearns for the simplicity of the tenth, the eighteenth, or even of the nineteenth centuries, and Thoreau's Walden Pond retreat would satisfy us for no longer than possibly a brief lakeside vacation. What this adds up to is that in the spontaneous judgment of most persons living in an era of technological advance *there has been progress.* This is not to say that there has been unadulterated progress, with all of life happier and better than before. Yet progress there has been in the satisfaction of human wants, and for this we may well thank God.

Yet we must not thank God in the spirit of the Pharisee. Perhaps the clearest evidence of the goodness of technology is the measure of longing for its fruits among the underprivileged peoples of the world. Where poverty, hunger, disease, illiteracy, and primitivism prevail, there the obligation rests upon the privileged to share as rapidly as possible the blessings of technology. Whether this be done through government-sponsored technical assistance, or vocational missions under church auspices, or through private enterprise, it must be done. It must be done for our security in a divided world, but apart from any political overtones in such economic aid it must be done for basic humanitarian and Christian reasons.

I have dwelt at some length on this first criterion of progress because it is both so evident and so important to the total life of man. But what of the second? Has technological advance been paralleled by what for want of a more explicit term goes by the ambiguous designation of *"culture"* or *"the good life"*?

In outlining these four principal criteria of progress, it was stated that the lines of distinction are blurred at the edges. This is evident in relation to this one. When one speaks of "gracious living" he usually means comfortable if not opulent living, with a number of slick magazines on the living room table, a television set in the corner, and around the house more than a few of the things advertised in both.

The term also connotes courtesy and a law-abiding respectability with at least a superficial politeness and the ability to get along with one's neighbors. To be a cultured person or family is to care about good manners, good schools, good music, art, dress, sports, or whatever else ranks high in the mores of the community. In short, it is practically synonymous with our secular culture.

Can we say that at this point also we have made progress? Certainly there is more of this kind of living than in the past. It is marked by careful attention to the needs and the pleasures of children, increased expenditures for the public schools, great interest at all ages in scientific knowledge, and much more attention to the diet, health, recreation, and social adjustment of both children and their elders than was formerly the case. While it blossoms most luxuriantly among the green lawns and split-level homes of the suburbs, few areas in the country are so remote, and few slum sections of the cities so squalid, that they are not in some measure touched by these marks of "the good society."

Yet are they really good? It is easy to point to broken homes, juvenile delinquency, an increase in the incidence of crime and of alcoholism, and widespread neurotic tension as evidences to the contrary. As was indicated in the previous chapter, it is doubtful that the rank and file of people today are happier than in the days of Puritan austerity, and perhaps they are less happy.

This, however, is not the real question. The good life ought to be happy, but happiness is not the criterion of the good life. Its more dependable criterion is the range and richness of its values. Is such modern living satisfactory from the standpoint of bodily and mental health, creativity and contentment in work and recreation, warmth of personal fellowship, opportunities for useful service at points of need? If so, it may not be the highest life, but it is good.

Viewed from this standpoint, our contemporary society is a great mixture. One can praise it or deplore it. One can find real elements of progress in rising levels of education, of health and longevity, of increased hours of leisure, of opportunities for creative self-expression. One can find also the killing demands of the work load in a competitive society and the still more exhausting and often frustrating burden of "keeping up with the Joneses." There is probably both more "togetherness" and more rootlessness today than in any preceding age.

Our net judgment is that according to this criterion also, as with the first, progress can be discerned. Yet it is a precarious progress. Can we not find something more dependable?

What of the third criterion, *growth in social organization* and the ability to live together harmoniously in widening social units? At first glance, this may seem a strange place to look for something less precarious and more stable than the preceding. The Cold War is a fearful reality, and nations threaten nations, with no clear answer to the tangled issues of either domestic or foreign policy.

Nevertheless, there has been real progress through the emergence of the nation state. With all the complexities that accompany political life in the twentieth century, we should not want to live in Plato's totalitarian Republic, or the stratified slave state of Aristotle. Nor should we want to live in England before the Magna Carta, or the American colonies before the Declaration of Independence. As region after region formerly a colonial possession comes to nationhood, as so many have in recent years, problems emerge; yet few persons among the democracies doubt that self-government and self-determination when properly prepared for are right and good.

Political freedom when it is linked with a concern for justice and the common good is a great ideal, with progress appearing wherever the ideal becomes the actual. What we must say in fidelity to the facts is that not only throughout the Communist world is such freedom lacking, but in much of the so-called free world it is severely circumscribed. Wherever race discrimination, economic injustice, or the denial of civil liberties exists, there progress is thwarted. One whose memory spans a half century can see considerable progress in America in the first two of these fields, rather less in the third, as fear mounts and freedom is exchanged for the hope of security. Both in race relations and in the just and harmonious adjustment of life to life and interest to interest in the world of work, wages, and prices, there is still a long way to go. Yet through gradual changes in community attitudes and through laws and their enforcement some headway has been made. We cannot claim any wholesale progress, but in such matters as desegregated schools, sports, employment, and health facilities and in the increased use of collective bargaining and arbitration for the redress of economic grievance, we are slowly moving forward. For such progress as appears, we must again thank God, and take courage for fresh effort.

But what of units of social organization beyond the nation state? In short, of the ability of nations to live together in a divided world? Here it is apparent that the world is in a more dangerous state than ever before, not because attitudes of suspicion and hostility are worse, but because the technical means of mutual destruction have been so vastly increased.

At this point, because of the extreme gravity of the present situation, it is easy to say that progress has reached its nadir. However, before we do, some considerations are in order. The first of these is the existence and the functioning of the United Nations, which in spite of its shortcomings and crippling vetoes continues to provide a sounding board for the moral sentiment of the world, renders great social services, and has repeatedly averted wars in trouble spots that without it would have burst into flames. A second major consideration is that both in spite of, and because of, this extreme danger of atomic destruction there is not likely to be a Third World War unless some accident or miscalculation unleashes it. And a third major consideration, perhaps the most important of the three, is that there was never a time when the masses of the world's people had so great a longing for peace and an awareness that it takes responsible citizenship, patient negotiation, and a curbing of the arms race—not military measures alone—to ensure our mutual security. The situation today is dark, but by no means is it *all* dark.

Accordingly, what we come out with in the third criterion of progress is that there has been genuine, though qualified, advance—an advance which it is impossible to measure quantitatively as greater or less, but within which there are rays of hope because of firmer foundations than in the days of a shallow optimism. Even through the darkness, God may be leading us to a better society.

The fourth criterion of progress is harder to define than the other three. If such progress exists, it is marked by *the increase of goodness in human nature and in human living.* This is something less tangible, and at the same time more basic, than advances in technology, culture, or international organization.

The possibility of defining progress by the increase of goodness is greatly complicated by the fact that there is no single, agreed-upon definition of goodness. There are various systems of both philosophical and Christian ethics, and there is a great deal of both moral and immoral living that proceeds without conscious relation to any kind of system. Yet goodness is not a blank, for we can and must keep thinking and talking about it.

Goodness cannot be defined legalistically or moralistically. Such affirmative and worthy indexes as being a good neighbor, engaging in regular church attendance, giving to good causes, or participating in worthwhile community enterprises are not enough to define it, for all these may be engaged in from unworthy motives. Still less is it possible to define it negatively as refraining from one or another of the things generally condemned by society, such as drunkenness, adultery, robbery, or murder. Yet we are not left without a basis for judgment, for goodness is discernible when we see it.

There is goodness outside the scope of Christianity, as the insights of the classical philosophers and the exponents of other high religions have long made evident. Without attempting to encompass all its expressions, it may be said to be characterized by a certain nobility of character in which courage, integrity, loyalty to ideals, and sensitivity to human values are outstanding virtues.

Christian goodness includes these virtues, and more, though it cannot be defined by any listing of a set of virtues. It is a quality of life which proceeds from the center outward.

Goodness at its highest is visible in the life lived by Jesus of Nazareth and set before his followers by both precept and example. It is marked by a deep trust in God and eagerness to do the will of God. At the heart of the will of God are love and compassion for all men, with an outgoing spirit of service which seeks out channels of helpfulness and asks no reward. In the inner life it is marked by sincerity, humility, repentance for sin, and confidence in the healing mercy of God by which one may go forward in newness of life. Paul long ago epitomized Christian goodness in nine terms that would be hard to improve upon. "But the fruit of the Spirit is love, joy, peace, patience, kindness, goodness, faithfulness, gentleness, self-control; against such there is no law." (Gal. 5:22-23.)

Is such goodness on the increase? I see no possibility of a quantitative measurement. There are both saints and sinners in every era in about constant proportions, and neither saintliness nor brutal rascality is nearly as common as is plain mediocrity.

But if goodness is not increasing, is sin becoming more virulent? There is an inborn self-centeredness in man which lies at the base of our self-righteous pride, acquisitiveness, hostility, aggressiveness, lust, inertia, and the hypocrisy by which to cover them.

This persistent sinfulness of the human self, unchanging from age to age though new forms of it emerge, has led many of today's theologians and social analysts to think darkly of the possibilities of human progress.

Granting the perennial sinfulness of the human ego, does the current scene reflect some significant conquest of these tendencies? If so, there would be real progress even if the stuff of man's biological inheritance remains unchanged. However, as life becomes more complex and more precarious, the disparity between Christian ideals of goodness and the state of society appears at some points to become the more glaring. A distinguished Christian statesman, Charles Malik, describes the contemporary scene in these vivid terms:

In the New Testament there are a dozen or more listings of the sins of that age. All these sins are rampant today. But we may add as peculiar to our age: drivenness, nervousness, fear, cowardice, rebelliousness, absence of rest and peace, flattening of thought and feeling, absence of the dimension of depth, innumerable new ways in which pleasure can be safely stolen, disintegration of community, massive irrationality and superstition, reliance upon speculation and chance, disdain of the law of cause and effect, weakening of the sense of personal responsibility, denial of the invisible and spiritual, the spread of militant atheism, the proud self-sufficiency of man.

As evidence that "this welter of sin" is not the whole story, Dr. Malik adds, "His is as heroic a life as any in history who emerges from all this welter of sin with the integrity of his soul not irreparably damaged and his heart still 'faithful to the heavenly vision.' With all his bruises he can at least trust himself to the mercy of God." [6]

[6] "The Burden of the Christian," *The Christian Century*, December 20, 1961, p. 1524. Used by permission.

The mercy of God! This is all-important when man's response is linked with it. We may well be grateful that this basic note in Christian faith, accented in the most fruitful days of the Christian faith and especially in the Protestant Reformation, is being so extensively recovered. Furthermore, with the prevalence of individual and social sin, it is still possible to witness triumphant Christian living. Those with lives centered in the love of God and service to others are not identical with the church members in official rosters. A large proportion of such Christians are unpretentious folk, unknown outside their own communities. Not a few of them are in remote lands, where to be a Christian and to affiliate with a minority movement is less popular and more costly than here.

Yet all over the world one finds them. The churches with all their shortcomings have fostered such Christian living, perhaps never more realistically than in the present. Both corporate worship and the personal devotional life are freshly accented. Christian education goes forward, with a firmer biblical, theological, and life-centered grounding than in the past. Theology and the study of the Bible are not only virile in the higher echelons of leadership, but laymen have a new interest in exploring the foundations of their faith, and the literature for this purpose is abundant.

The missionary movement has spread the Christian gospel around the world, generating strong indigenous leadership in many parts of it. It continues to do so in spite of obstacles, to such an extent that in the total scene this may constitute our major hope of Christian progress.[7] The ecumenical movement unites Christians across denominational lines and in many nations and

[7] This is the conclusion stated by John Baillie in *The Belief in Progress,* Chapter V.

cultures in significant programs of study and action. Spearheaded by this movement, but arising out of the dislocations and turmoil of the Second World War, a new awareness of the indispensable work of the laity has arisen. Laymen are discovering that they are not simply assistants to the clergy in the organizational activities of the churches, but that they are the church within the world with a ministry to the world in the vocations of daily life.

I speak primarily as a Protestant Christian. Yet similar movements of advance are to be found within Roman Catholicism, in part spearheaded by the magnanimous spirit of Pope John XXIII and the Second Vatican Council, in part independent developments among concerned leaders. Never has the cordiality between the theologians and ecclesiastical leaders of these two great groups of Christians been as warm as it is today. Advance within the churches does not guarantee the spiritual advance of individual Christians, but it opens the door.

Thus it appears that dissension, strife, and sin are not the only notes of our time. Furthermore, they are not the major notes. Unity is in the air. There is a greater striving for international cooperation and world peace, for racial equality and harmony, for missionary and ecumenical advance, for meaningful corporate worship, for healthy personal adjustment, for understanding of the Christian faith, for Christian fellowship across lines of separation, than has been witnessed in this conjunction in any previous era. Perhaps such a combination of lines of advance would not have been possible in smoother times. In any case, the urgency of the times has stirred such movements to a new vitality.

The net result of our study this far is that the question, "Can we believe in progress?" cannot be answered with an unequivocal Yes or No. There has been enough advance along numerous lines

to give encouragement; yet the preservation and increase of
these points of advance is not so certain as to justify complacency.

We must now probe somewhat deeper, and ask on what foundations such assurance as we have can safely rest. Are they part
of a larger purpose? And do these grounds give hope for the
future?

3. Unsatisfactory views of progress

We are now in a position to make some assessment of true and
false views of progress. In order to end the chapter on a constructive note we shall look first at certain interpretations of progress
which ought without qualification to be rejected. Their general
rejection may therefore be regarded as a gain.

One of these we have already noted—that as the generations
come and go, man's natural impulses to sin become less virulent.
This view has not been widely held, but in the heyday of the
impact of biological evolution some attempts were made to affirm a corresponding moral and intellectual advance in the human species. There is so little evidence to support it that it is now
seldom advocated. Its "opposite number" is the lauding of primitivism, the glorification of the life of the "noble savage," a yearning for return to an age of innocence. The more one learns of
anthropological fact and the sweep of history, the less one sees of
evidence to support either of these positions. The spirit of man
has always been sinful, even as human life has always been
precarious. The forms of sinning and the sources of anxiety
change, but not man's basic predicament.

Yet if it be granted that there has been no biological advance or
retrogression within the human species, this does not prove that
there has been no social evolution. This is the more crucial ques-

tion, for it is around this issue that most of the defense or denial of progress has centered.

In the earlier part of this chapter evidences were cited to show that whichever criterion is appealed to, there have been forms of progress in human society. This is not to claim unadulterated progress, or to attempt to balance in any quantitative fashion the degree of advance with the emergence of new problems. The more modest claim was simply to show that enough progress has occurred to call forth gratitude to God and afford some grounds of hope for the future.

Yet to affirm any social progress at all is to open the door to false interpretations of it. At some of these we must now look.

The most conspicuous of these false and hence overoptimistic views was the belief in *inevitable—sometimes termed automatic —progress*. It was never widely held in the churches, though it is now often castigated as having been a primary tenet of liberal theology. Where it was advocated on religious grounds, this was sometimes due to overconfidence in scientific intelligence and social engineering, a confidence borrowed from the secular climate of the day. It was more often the product of faith in a divine Providence, epitomized in the words,

> One God, one law, one element,
> And one far-off divine event,
> To which the whole creation moves.[8]

Of this faith we shall have more to say in the next section.

Nevertheless, in the nineteenth and early twentieth centuries, the belief in inevitable progress was quite widely held in secular intellectual circles. This rested on several foundations, and as

---

[8] Tennyson, "In Memoriam."

the foundations tottered the belief was also shaken, either to
the point of collapse or of serious question.

The first of these foundations was the obviously great achievements of human reason, knowledge, and skills in the natural
sciences. Since these achievements continue without interruption,
there are still those who believe that they are bound to lead to human happiness and the good life. Yet, with the growing complex-
ity of the economic and political problems of our time, it has become evident to most persons that technological advance does
not inevitably produce either inner or outer security.

In both minor and major matters every advance brings new
problems. As automobiles increase, so does the parking problem.
As goods become more plentiful, installment buying and debt
create new worries. As infant mortality declines, overpopulation
grows. As the life-span lengthens through medical care, new
problems both *for* and *about* the older generation emerge.

That there is a glaring discrepancy between the tools available
for satisfactory living and its achievement is a common theme in
current literature. To cite an example, both the title and the content of John Steinbeck's novel *The Winter of Our Discontent*
illustrate it. Its principal character is being chided for being
"knocked out." He replies:

Men . . . can fight back against big things. What kills them is
erosion; they get nudged into failure. They get slowly scared. I'm
scared. Long Island Lighting Company might turn off the lights. My
wife needs clothes. My children—shoes and fun, and . . . education.
And the monthly bills and the doctor and teeth and a tonsillectomy . . .
and suppose I get sick? Course you don't understand. It rots your
guts away. I can't think beyond next month's payment on the re-
frigerator. I hate my job and I'm scared I'll lose it.[9]

[9] (New York: Viking Press, 1961), p. 13.

With this a prevalent mood, inevitable progress has few defenders.

A somewhat more sophisticated ground of faith in assured social progress is the deterministic view that human society can be indefinitely remade to become what it ought to be through human engineering. This has its roots in the sociological doctrine, first promulgated by Auguste Comte who gave it the name of positivism, that by discovering and applying certain positive laws of society, all social evils can eventually be corrected. This is the foundation on which many social services rest, with enough realism in the fact that known causes bring predictable effects to make it a useful basis of action. Yet if the deterministic view is held consistently, as it usually is not, its implications run counter to human freedom. The human spirit resents manipulation, and asserting itself in selfishness and inertia, it refuses to be made over. There is little evidence of the probable creation through social control of any such general benevolence as would guarantee social progress.

A third ideological support for a doctrine of inevitable progress emerged in the nineteenth century through a combination of influential philosophical currents. Herbert Spencer's doctrine of evolution, even before Darwin, gave a great impetus to the expectancy of a continuing forward movement, and became blended in many minds with the Darwinian doctrine of natural selection after the latter emerged. In the same century the Hegelian philosophy of absolute idealism, with its philosophy of history as the unfolding of the currents of destiny in a pattern of thesis, antithesis, and synthesis, gave grounds for holding that evil elements were only temporary and were bound to give way to a greater good. Although biological evolution, chiefly associated with the name of Charles Darwin though developed by many, is now accepted as scientific certainty, none of these philosophies is any longer widely current. As they have faded out, so has the doctrine of progress associated with them.

Even without these changes in philosophical climate, the course of events would have raised serious questions about the optimistic hopes of an earlier day. The coming of two World Wars in one generation, with a gigantic depression and the outcroppings of Nazi tyranny and brutality between them, was more influential than the philosophers, social scientists, or theologians in shattering popular hopes. Even before the rise of communism as a menace to free societies throughout the world, or the emergence of the horrible possibilities of nuclear destruction, history had put a quietus on trust in inevitable progress.

A more common ground of optimism at present in secular and sometimes in religious thought is the view that progress, though uneven, is sufficiently *cumulative* to give assurance of moving forward. It roots in the assumption that though advance comes by streaks and patches, with recessions now and then, the ground is not really lost. This view is not perfectionist in the sense of looking forward to any utopia, and it appeals to those who are willing to settle for less than perfection provided the general trend is forward. An example is the faith of those who believe that the American economy, though occasional recessions are to be expected, is bound to recover and advance. There is a comparable faith in the American educational system in spite of its admitted defects.

It is more difficult to speak categorically about this than about the preceding views that have been termed false, for it is partly true and partly false. The true element lies in the fact that with any objective backward look, cumulative progress in education, knowledge, skills, productivity, transportation, communication, health, living conditions, and the generally accepted standards of a civilized culture can be discerned.

Yet it is not enough to stop at this point. Can we be sure that such progress up to the present will continue? May we not have reached the peak, from which the probable future course is descent or collapse? May not our civilization, like the twenty-five before it of which Arnold Toynbee writes,[10] be headed for dissolution?

If the belief in cumulative progress is held to as assured sociological fact, it must be viewed as very questionable. Though it claims less than the belief in inevitable progress, it rests on an equally precarious view of human relations. If it stands at all, it must find its rootage in other soil. For the present we shall leave it at that, and turn to the grounds of optimism that were prevalent in the heyday of theological liberalism.

Faith in inevitable progress on scientific or sociological or ideological grounds was false; it deserved to die. But were there also false views among the exponents of Christian faith?

I have already said that I do not believe that faith in inevitable progress was ever widely held among religious leaders. Nevertheless, there was a somewhat related faith, usually now referred to as utopian, which was in better standing. It was tied in with the thought of *the coming of the kingdom of God upon earth*. It drew its origin from the belief that it was not enough to pray, "Thy kingdom come. Thy will be done on earth, as it is in heaven." Pray for it we must; but we must also work for it, wait for it, and expect it. In general, only the Adventists and other premillenarians believed it was coming soon, but many liberals

[10] *The Study of History* (London and New York: Oxford University Press, 1939), IV, 1. Of these twenty-five, Toynbee says that sixteen are already dead, the other nine are in various stages of disintegration and threat of assimilation by the civilization of the West.

at opposite poles from them in general theological outlook believed it was coming with certainty on earth. This was almost always conceived as a reformed and purified society rather than
as the second coming of Christ.

This was usually accompanied by a strong sense of the Christian's obligation to do what he could to correct the evils of society
for the advancement of the kingdom. While again I do not believe that the characteristic thrust of this movement was as man-
centered and self-righteous as it is now decried for being, it was
certainly associated in many minds with the idea of "building" the
kingdom. The fact that this phrase still survives in the diction of
many middle-aged and older Christian leaders indicates its wide
acceptance.

However, more important than particular terms is the fact that
persons committed to this outlook believed that God was calling
them to act to make this a better world. The social gospel was central to Christian ethics.

Was this a false perspective? In part, it was; in other aspects,
decidedly not.

What was false about it was the utopian note that crept in
through an underrating of the power of sin in individual and social life. Genuine victories over evil in both spheres led to the
belief that not only was such victory possible, but that in some
indefinite future—"in God's good time," but as a consequence of
faithful and determined human effort—the victory was assured.

Today the trend of Christian thought has shifted to a more
modest expectation, based on a more realistic appraisal of man's
possibilities. As long as human nature continues to be sinful and
finite, the perfect society will not come on earth—and there is no
indication that sin and finitude will cease. Therefore, though
the coming of the kingdom is in God's hands, and it is not for us

to know the times and the seasons, it is improbable that the kingdom will ever fully come on earth.

So far, this curtailment of man's overoptimistic expectations is a gain. We can work more soberly and realistically if we do not expect too much, and to rely more on the wisdom and strength of God than on our own is Christian humility. What is regrettable, however, is that so much of the imperative to labor for a better society seems to have waned with the passing of this earlier view. The social gospel does not need to depend on a false utopianism; it ought to go forward in greater strength when freed from error. Nevertheless, its disparagement today is in no slight degree connected with the surrender of the hope for the coming of the kingdom in human society. To preserve the gain without this loss is imperative.

We have looked now at a number of untenable views of progress. We shall try in the next section to suggest some true elements in the Christian position on which we have the right—indeed, the duty—to confront the future with hope.

4. Firmer foundations

Fundamental to any true Christian belief in progress is faith in divine providence. Providence, as I have attempted to state at length in another book,[11] does not mean that God predestines every event. It does not mean that every event is just as God would have it, or that it is to be viewed as in some mysterious way good because God caused it. To say that every tragedy and frustration in human life, to say nothing of every act of human sin, is the will of God is little short of blasphemy. To believe in Providence, on the contrary, is to believe that in every human

---

[11] *The Providence of God* (Nashville: Abingdon Press, 1960).

situation, however stark, bleak, and evil it may actually be, God in his compassionate love offers guidance and strength and seeks to make good come out of evil.

To speak of God's providence is to suggest his concern for every individual human life, and without such belief in God's loving care for individuals the heart of the doctrine is lost. God does not love the human race en masse, but Person to person. From this conviction the possibility of prayer, gratitude, and trust becomes credible.

Yet God is concerned with the currents of society as well. In this connection we more commonly speak of him as the Lord of history. To believe in God's providential leading and care of individuals is to believe also that he is related to human society, since societies exist by the meshing together of the lives of a great number of individuals. To believe that God is no static Absolute Being, but Infinite Love that cares what happens to persons in their time-bound lives, is also to believe that the eternal God is concerned about and has a purpose for the total movement of human history. God from this perspective cannot be indifferent to human progress.

If we hold this faith, there is no reason to lift a sophisticated eyebrow and brand as "Victorian" such a couplet as this:

Yet I doubt not thro' the ages one increasing purpose runs,
And the thoughts of men are widen'd with the process of the suns.[12]

The surest ground we have for belief in progress is that God does have "one increasing purpose," increasing for men as our apprehensions and capacities grow through a better use of God's gifts, but constant in God's intention and design.

[12] Tennyson, "Locksley Hall."

What is this purpose? As far as we can know it through God's revelation of himself in Jesus Christ, it is the increase of love of God and neighbor with an ever-widening mutual helpfulness and upbuilding in the things that make for richness of personal self-hood. There is no list of things that will define it, but we see it in the ministry and words, the life and death, of Jesus. We see it reflected, clouded but still discernible, in the lives of persons unmistakably Christian who have blessed and touched our lives.

We cannot define progress by saying that there is more saintliness now than in previous centuries. Saintliness like sin remains fairly constant. Saintliness is as rare, even as sin is as common, in one generation as the next. Nevertheless, what we can say is that the will of God is progressively discerned as men advance in spiritual insight, and that this is true not only in individual lives but as advances occur in the stream of history from primitive gropings to the insights of high religions.

But what of society as a whole? Is the Lord of history leading us forward?

What was said earlier about the falsity of belief in inevitable progress must not here be retracted. Faith in divine providence does not guarantee social progress, for God has endowed men with freedom of choice and decision. In defiance of God's will this freedom is too often expressed in acts and attitudes of selfish pride, hostility, passive indifference, and active hatred. By such human willfulness social progress is thwarted, and human history *may* end in mutual destruction.

Nevertheless, faith in divine providence gives stable grounds for hope. Not the least of these is what may seem at first glance like its opposite—the linkage of divine providence with divine judgment. God does not permit evil to thrive with impunity. God has placed within his universe a moral order—an order as real, though not so precisely predictable, as the natural order on which science rests. Apparently the world is meant to be a family, with its human members living together not only in peace but in mutual goodwill and helpfulness. Where this occurs, everybody gains in happiness and well-being, and progress takes place which must rejoice the heart of the Almighty. Where this world-familiness is thwarted, conflict breaks out and everybody loses.

Thus, the suffering that ensues when men's acts are counter to the ways of God, though it often seems unjust and ought never to be gloried in, is in a deep sense a blessing. It is disciplinary, and it can be redemptive. Without the penalties that follow on the heels of social sin, the challenge to repentance and renewal would seem far less urgent. Accepted in the spirit of humility, trust, and obedient response which we learn from Jesus Christ, it can lead to both individual and social newness of life.

At this point the cryptic words of Joseph to his brethren become relevant. "As for you, you meant evil against me; but God meant it for good." (Gen. 50:20.) It is impossible to place on God the responsibility for human sin. Yet again and again in retrospect it is possible to see that good has come out of some evil thing, either through the challenge to action in recoil from it or through the sheer fact that the evil wears itself out until the good triumphs. I do not believe that we can count automatically on the self-destructiveness of evil, but it happens too often to be disregarded. It could happen to either of the twin evils of nuclear war and communist tyranny if the burden became too great for human acceptance.

In the previous section we left somewhat suspended the question of cumulative progress, stating that hope based upon it was unstable when affirmed as sociological fact but might have deeper roots. These roots now become visible. By faith we may affirm that no good deed, done in love and in obedience to the call of God, is ever wholly futile. No good results may be evident to human eyes, or such results as the touching of an individual human life here and there may seem quite inconsequential. There is no precise formula by which to measure the fruits of effort in the realm of such intangibles, and the cause to which we give ourselves with deep devotion may seem as lost as the cause of Jesus on the day after the crucifixion. Nevertheless, in God's economy no deed done in love and obedience is ever wasted effort.

Effort in infinitely varied ways is called for. Nobody can do everything, and each must find his vocation—his particular calling from God in conjunction with opportunity and talent. If there is to be any outer progress, the inner lives of people must be ministered to and stabilized by deeper spiritual resources. It is equally true that the social chains that pin men down must be lifted by steady, wise, courageous effort. Clergy and laity and those outside the churches—all of us—must do it together.

So we are brought to this conclusion. The Lord of history would have us move forward in closer cooperation, in deeper respect for one another and for the good things of life that all men ought to have, in greater love and mutual helpfulness. To this end he calls us to repentance, forgives us in mercy, empowers us to act in obedient service. Social progress occurs; it has occurred; it will occur through human effort, for God does not bring it to pass without our cooperation. Yet any progress that is more than artificial glitter is the gift of God. Stripped of self-righteous pride in human achievement we should be grateful for it, and expect hopefully to go forward.

Both within the turmoil of our world and through a higher

purpose that transcends it, we may believe that God is preparing
us providentially for better days to come. And whatever the future
holds, whether from the human point of viewing brighter times
or deeper darkness, God is still Sovereign of our world, and no
man need despair.

IV

THE BIBLICAL
VIEW OF HISTORY

THE CONCLUSION TO WHICH THE PREVIOUS CHAPTER
led is that the "evolutionary optimism" of the late nineteenth and
early twentieth centuries died of its own weight of error, and
can no longer be defended on either historical or theological
grounds. Nevertheless, this does not automatically banish belief
in progress, any more than earlier naturalistic assumptions automatically guaranteed it. What survives is the evidence that in
many aspects of human existence progress has occurred, though
never as an unmixed forward movement, and that its ultimate
explanation is to be found in divine providence rather than in
natural or human causation as the last word. It is in this providence and man's obedient response that our hope is grounded.

Let us close this phase of our discussion, and begin the next,
with two quotations from a foremost contemporary philosopher
of history, Herbert Butterfield:

So far as I can see, one's ultimate values—or the general meaning
of life—can never be based on the idea of progress, which affects not
man himself but the framework and the conditions of life. But I think
that I may differ from some people in feeling that progress all the
same is itself the work of Providence, and is part of that providential
order, part of that history-making which goes on almost, so to speak,
above our heads.[1]

[1] *Christianity and History* (New York: Charles Scribner's Sons, 1950),
p. 96.

89

This semiwhimsical affirmation of a profound truth is reinforced later by a word of utter seriousness.

Providence . . . is not a thing to be presumed upon; and indeed the Christian knows that it gives him no guarantee against martyrdom for the faith. What it does guarantee so exultantly in the New Testament is a mission in the world and the kind of triumph that may come out of apparent defeat—the kind of good that can be wrested out of evil.[2]

The belief in Providence is a vital aspect of the biblical view of history or, more accurately, of the suprahistorical as it impinges on and gives meaning to human history. Yet it is not the only aspect. Other aspects were passed over with brief mention and the promise that more would be said about them later. The biblical view of history, accordingly, is the theme of this chapter. The kingdom of God, both within history and beyond it, will be our subject in the next.

1. What is history?

The term "history" is a somewhat ambiguous one. It can mean anything that happens in time, including physical nature as well as man. In this sense we can speak of geological history, the history of the solar system, or even of the cosmos as a whole. More commonly, history as a social science, as distinguished from the natural or the biological sciences, centers in *human* events and processes, however much these may be affected by natural or biological forces. In theological diction, where it is essential to talk of time and eternity, of the life on earth and whatever lies beyond it, history refers usually to what happens to man on earth, with eschatology—the doctrine of the "last things"—as its

[2] *Ibid.*, p. 112.

contrasting term. Within these distinctions still another must be
drawn, for history can mean all human events on earth, known
or unknown, remembered or forgotten, or it can mean the knowledge of recorded or remembered events in contrast with what is
prehistoric or unnoticed. And, to restrict the term still further,
events that "make history" are those of outstanding significance
which greatly influence the subsequent course of human events.

All of these meanings are legitimate in context, with what
happens to man in time and on earth as a common center of all
but the first. We shall use the term in this inclusive sense unless
some other meaning seems to be called for by the matter under
discussion.

Yet we cannot leave the definition of the meaning of history
without another differentiation which is extremely crucial, not
only to biblical history but to all history. This is the distinction
which Richard Niebuhr drew in his illuminating book *The Meaning of Revelation;* namely, the difference between external and
internal history. External history, which might also be called objective or scientific history, is the record of events just as they
actually occurred, or as close an approximation to such accuracy
as the fullest use of investigation and research can ascertain. It
is much more than the "bare bones" of names and dates, for it
involves the tracing of causal sequences to determine the geographical, economic, sociological, or psychological factors which
caused the events to happen, and, in turn, how social groups
were affected by these events as their political and economic
conditions and patterns of behavior were altered.

Internal history, on the other hand, centers in the meaning of
these events for one whose life has been gripped by them. There
is a history *as seen* and a history *as lived,* and it is the latter that
constitutes internal history. Niebuhr cites as an illustration the

difference between a scientific case history of the restoration of
sight in a blind man by surgery and what an autobiography will
recount of what had happened to a self that had lived in darkness and now saw again trees and the sunrise, children's faces
and the eyes of a friend. In a social milieu, internal history is
that which is *ours*, and which we believe in, as Lincoln believed
in the history and destiny of America when he gave the Gettys-
burg Address, history which "calls for joy and sorrow, for days of
rededication and of shriving, for tragic participation and for
jubilees." [3]

Such internal history is in a sense subjective. Whether one
celebrates the exodus from Egypt, the Feast of Lights, the birth,
death, and resurrection of Jesus, the signing of the Declaration
of Independence, the harvest festival of our Pilgrim fathers, the
protest of Martin Luther, or the conversion of John Wesley depends on whether one stands within the tradition where these
events are meaningful. The experience must become *mine* to
sense the drama and the greatness of it. Yet in all the major
events it is also *ours*. Remembered history is the history of a people, not of a solitary individual.

Objective and internal history are not in conflict, for internal
history rests on the foundation of events that really happened.
Their exact nature may not be known, and the story may be told
in imaginative, even "mythological," form. Yet this is quite different from fiction—a story dreamed up out of somebody's imagination which has no basis in fact. Internal history, to be lasting
and meaningful, must be historical, and not solely psychological.

Yet neither can external history take the place of internal his-

[3] H. Richard Niebuhr, *The Meaning of Revelation* (New York: The Macmillan Company, 1941), pp. 60, 68.

tory. Whether we are speaking of such events as the death of Socrates, the birth of Lincoln, the granting of the Magna Carta, or the landing of the Pilgrims on Plymouth Rock, what objectively occurred cannot be dissociated from the meaning that has become attached to the event. Furthermore, external history, since it lies in the past, is in a sense dead, gone, and finished, while internal history is the living and continuous—or at least the repeated—reenactment of its meaning. The Last Supper occurred but once; the Lord's Supper has brought a poignant and sacred memory innumerable times to innumerable hosts of Christians.

Thus far I have made no attempt to relate the meaning of internal history to the biblical view except to suggest by some illustrations that it shares the common characteristics of other remembered events. It at once becomes apparent, however, that the interdependence of external and internal history is directly related to the question of whether the "Christ of faith" can replace the "Jesus of history." Christian faith comes to us in a long tradition, mediated to us through the Christian community, and many of its affirmations are bound to seem unpersuasive, if not meaningless, to those who stand outside this community. Does this mean that the Bible ought to be, or can be, "demythologized" to suit the modern scientific mood? How much external history must be preserved if the internal history is to be nourished? These are questions which are at the focus of contemporary Christian thought. However, I shall attempt no answer to them until some other aspects of the biblical view of history are presented.

One other aspect, though a related one, may be touched upon before we move ahead. Does history consist only of remembered or recorded events, capable of producing high moments when we think of them? In an old but still valuable collection of essays, published under the title *The Kingdom of God and History*, written in preparation for the Oxford Conference of 1937 on Church, Community, and State, Paul Tillich defines history as the "totality of remembered events, which are determined by free human activity and are important for the life of human groups." [4] In terms of what has just been said about internal history (though Tillich does not use this term), it is clear that such events must be "remembered" and must seem "important" to human groups. One is reminded of the definition of the church given by John Knox as the "community which remembers Jesus." [5]

Still the need for an event to be remembered in order to find a place in history leaves me somewhat unsatisfied. Along with the famous personalities and the crucial events of which the historian must speak, human history has embraced a far greater number of ordinary persons doing ordinary things, enduring pain, experiencing occasional moments of happiness, meeting life as it comes with boredom, rebellion, endurance, or satisfaction. An essential aspect of the Christian view of history is that such persons, though nameless and unknown except to God and to those nearest them, *become* important through the love of God. History in the fullest sense must embrace the lives and experiences of all persons, not alone the remembered few.

So, we come back to what was stated earlier—that, unless there is some occasion to use the term in a different context, we shall speak of history as what happens to mankind in time and on earth, though certainly there are special events of unusual significance within such happenings. What, then, is the biblical view of history?

[4] *Op. cit.*, p. 110.
[5] *The Man Christ Jesus* (Chicago: Willett, Clark & Company, 1941), p. 18.

2. Essential notes in the biblical view

The purpose of this section will be to state in somewhat summary fashion the dominant characteristics of the biblical view of man's life within the currents of history. A later section will take up the permanent significance of certain basic biblical notes.

a) To the biblical writers, *history moves forward.* It drives toward goals. We have noted the characteristic Greek tendency, imported into the book of Ecclesiastes, to view life as a great recurrent wheel. In this round of existence, both the hedonistic note of "eat, drink, and be merry, for tomorrow we die," and the stark, inexorable fatalities of Greek tragedy are located. In the Hinduism and Buddhism of the present there is still much of the same note of an endless, wearisome "wheel of rebirth." The lovely temples and pagodas of the Far East are houses of refuge from life's struggle far more than they are a summons to hopeful activity and zeal for the conquest of life's woes. Even the half-humorous, half-compassionate smile on the face of the great stone Buddhas suggests both the irony of existence and pity for the victims of it, but no escape save in Nirvana. In the religions of the Orient, except as Christianity or Islam have entered this area, there is little or nothing of an onward, forward movement on the plane of history.

All this is radically different in the Judeo-Christian tradition insofar as it keeps to its biblical roots. The drama begins in creation for a purpose, with the delegation to man of stewardship over the created world. This passes rapidly into the covenant made by God with his chosen people, whereby hopefully by obedience they may merit the divine favor. When disobedience ensues and judgment falls upon the nation, they are still not left without hope, for God through his prophets promises the deliverer. This promise comes to fulfillment in the coming of Christ, though not in the ways most commonly expected. With his death and resurrection the church comes into being through the Holy Spirit. The Bible ends with the community of Christ's followers still facing forward, enduring persecution in the hope of a more glorious "new heaven and new earth" beyond the realm of earthly history.

b) *The Bible is not a book of philosophy but of "God's mighty acts."* Although Job, Proverbs, and Ecclesiastes are designated as "wisdom literature," none of the three is philosophy in the sense of a theoretical inquiry into the nature of existence, and none of the other sixty-three books approximates it. There is wisdom throughout the Bible, but it is the wisdom born of seeing, feeling, and telling about the acts of God in his righteous, gracious dealings with his people in judgment and redemption.

Accordingly, the Bible abounds in events which become "internal history." The thoughtful modern Jew sees his own sufferings and accomplishments in the light of God's covenant with Abraham, the Egyptian servitude, Moses the deliverer from bondage and the transmitter of the law, the conquest of Canaan, the glory and decline of David's kingdom, the exile, and the return to reestablish the Temple and the law. The Christian carries along these events, but finds greater inspiration in the coming of Christ and the treasured memories of his birth, his ministry of teaching and healing, his death and glorious resurrection. In the establishment of the church and the commission to witness to all nations, the worldwide outreach of Christian faith is grounded.

c) In the biblical perspective, *all history is an encounter between men and God.* It is a sphere in which man meets God—to use a somewhat overworked modern term—in an "I-Thou" relation, not in any detached sense as an onlooker. God ordains the situation in which man finds himself; God requires of man obedience to his will; God feels both wrath and sorrow over man's sin; God speaks the words of judgment and redemption. Man may deny his involvements, but he is still involved in responsible decision. Man may seek to flee from God's presence, but neither heaven nor Sheol, the wings of the morning nor the uttermost parts of the sea, will hide him from God.

d) *History focuses in the present moment of decision.* The memory of events may stretch backward to the beginnings of creation, and anticipation may encompass not only the end of history but what lies beyond it. Yet there is no escape by looking backward or forward from responsible decision *now*. This is epitomized in the familiar word from the book of Deuteronomy: "See, I have set before you this day life and good, death and evil. . . . I call heaven and earth to witness against you this day, that I have set before you life and death, blessing and curse; therefore choose life, that you and your descendants may live" (30:15, 19). This is implied throughout the Bible, and no Shakespearean "tomorrow, and tomorrow, and tomorrow" accords with the Bible's mood. This is no accident, for Macbeth's judgment that life

is a tale
Told by an idiot, full of sound and fury,
Signifying nothing

is as far removed as anything could be from the Bible's basic presuppositions.

e) *History is a social, or communal, enterprise.* This is not to say that there is no concern for the individual, for by the Bible's overtones every person is made in the divine image and is precious to God, even as every person is morally responsible and every person sins. Yet the general presupposition is not of the individual alone before God, as in the mystical, Neoplatonic "flight of the alone to the Alone" of Plotinus and many later mystics. Rather, God's encounter is with the individual in community—the community of the nation in the Old Testament and in the New, the community of Christ's followers in the church. This does not absolve the individual of responsibility either for his devotional life or for the life of action, and it is significant that most of the psalms, unlike our hymns of today, are written in the first person singular. Nevertheless, the presupposition of the biblical view of man's relation to God is of a supporting and demanding community—a community through which God speaks to the individual in a corporate relation, and a community about which God cares mightily.

f) The purposes of God, both for the individual and the community, are at the same time hidden and revealed. The stress is laid first on the one side of this paradox, then on the other, for both sides are present.

> Can you find out the deep things of God?
>   Can you find out the limit of the Almighty?
> It is higher than heaven—what can you do?
>   Deeper than Sheol—what can you know? (Job 11:7-8.)

Yet the prophet could speak with the assurance of "thus saith the Lord," and Jesus astonished his contemporaries, for "he taught them as one who had authority, and not as their scribes" (Matt. 7:29). The biblical writers never attributed to even the greatest of their lawgivers, kings, or sages the wisdom of God. Yet to those of the New Testament "Christ the power of God and the wisdom of God" (I Cor. 1:24) has drawn aside the veil. Whatever else may enter into the various forms of Christology by which men seek to define the person and work of Christ, his revelation of God's purpose as centering in self-giving love is seldom questioned.

g) Finally, *history is the primary medium of revelation*. This has been presupposed in saying that the Bible has no place for theoretical philosophizing and little for solitary encounter with God outside the community of faith. Nevertheless, it must be emphasized that the Bible's mode of divine disclosure is a Person-to-person meeting within the events of human living. Some, though not all, of these events were luminous moments that greatly affected the future, like Moses' encounter on Sinai, Isaiah's vision in the Temple, the Last Supper in the upper room, the coming of the Spirit on the day of Pentecost. Others were more "ordinary." These particular ones were times of temporary withdrawal from daily demands, as ours must be in the rhythm of work and worship. Yet they were not withdrawals from history, and their consequences in history were enormous.

However much the teller of the tale in retrospect may have added imaginative, pictorial, and unscientific details to the story, the event itself rests on a solid basis of human experience within the stream of history. Because it does, it kindles the heart to the present day. Any merely fanciful item, such as that of a speaking ass or a talking serpent, fails to do so.

Thus we come out with the belief that the "Christ of faith" compels belief in the "Jesus of history"—not in a first-century Jew of whom a fully accurate biography can be written, but the Jesus we know through what the record tells us of what he *said* and *did*. And because we thus know him, though we do not know all about him, we can say with the centurion who witnessed his death, "Truly this man was a son of God" (Mark 15:39).

Historical revelation comes to its climax in the Incarnation. It is because "we have beheld his glory, glory as of the only Son from the Father," that we believe in Jesus Christ as the Word made flesh. On any other ground the word "incarnation" is self-contradictory and meaningless.

3. History and myth

Since the appearance of Rudolf Bultmann's essay on *Kerygma and Myth*, translated into English in 1953, there is no problem which has so occupied the center of theological attention as his proposal for "demythologizing" the Bible, and especially the New Testament, to make its message more accessible to modern man. We cannot here go into all the arguments that have been put forth on both sides of the question. It may, however, provide a first step toward a discussion of it to define what we mean by myth. It is a term that is by no means clear and unambiguous.

There are various kinds of myth, and in the present writer's judgment some should, and others should not, be demythologized.

There is, first, the mythology that is simply folklore. In this class I would put the speaking ass (Num. 22:28-30) and the talking serpent (Gen. 3:1-5), although, as in the story of the Fall, one element of a story may be of this type without vitiating the profound meaning in the myth as a whole. Such folklore, if it means nothing in particular, we need not hesitate to bypass; for example, Gen. 6:1-4, which tells us that "the Nephilim [giants] were on the earth in those days, and also afterward, when the sons of God came in to the daughters of men, and they bore children to them." Such demigods were common enough in pagan mythology, but they do not belong in Judaism or Christianity.

A second kind of mythology is the vast array of stories found in the blending of religion with culture in the early stages of virtually every civilization. Such stories are not historical in the objective sense, although much of the people's folkways, and what

they believed about themselves, the universe, and their relation
to it can be detected by the discerning social scientist. Illustrations outside the Bible are the doings of the gods in the Greek
pantheon; the creation myth in Babylonia which tells of the
titanic struggle of Marduk with the dragon Tiamat; in Hinduism
the story of Brahma breathing in and out the created universe;
the Egyptian sun myth, picturing Ra as crossing the firmament in
a boat. Others, like the myth of Romulus and Remus, celebrate
national beginnings. Such myths are more than simple folklore,
for they attempt to answer serious questions. Yet they are neither
history nor philosophy. Emerging from the collective conscious-
ness of a dim past, they have no special authorship.

A third type of myth is an intentional literary form, used by an
author who knows that he is telling a fanciful story for the sake
of conveying an idea. It contains pictorial imagery which, if skill-
fully presented, conveys meaning more effectively than a more
matter-of-fact presentation. An example of this type is the myth
of the soul in Plato's *Phaedrus,* wherein the charioteer (reason)
drives a pair of white and black winged horses (the higher moral
qualities and the appetites) and tries to mount up to heaven, but
ends by falling to earth and entering into man. Neither Plato nor
anyone else took this to be history, but its meaning has been
discussed for many centuries.

There is still a fourth type of myth which has a foundation in
history. It was told in the beginning as objective fact, but in the
telling it has gathered about it the accretions arising from "internal history." Its foundation is true; its meaning is true; its
form does not meet the present-day canons of scientific proba-
bility.

In my judgment, a great deal of the discussion of demythologizing has been at cross purposes through failure to distinguish be-

tween these various kinds of myth. In trying to understand the Bible, what shall we do with each type?

The first type, scattered here and there, and found especially in the Bible's earliest writings, is of no special consequence except that it shows us these writers as human beings enmeshed in the culture of their times. It is of more importance to anthropology than to religion.

The second type is of much greater importance. To it belong the myths of the Creation and the Fall, the Flood and the Tower of Babel. In some respects they resemble their Babylonian counterparts, though on a much higher level of spiritual insight. They carry a profound meaning, though in a completely pre-scientific, nonhistorical setting. We do well to demythologize them, so long as we preserve their meaning as to God the ultimate Creator, man the inveterate sinner, the fruits of disobedience, and the God who makes an everlasting covenant of grace with man in spite of his sin.

As for the third type, consciously designed by an author to convey meaning in pictorial form, the Bible contains no philosophic myths, unless the dramatic setting of the book of Job is thus considered. It has many parables and some allegories, but these are not myths. The nearest approach to intentional mythology is in the apocalyptic symbolism of Daniel and Revelation. Such symbolism and the language of vision is not history, but it has its setting within a historical situation.

Recognized for what it is—a literary form used to convey a message of challenge, comfort, and hope through the assurance of God's everpresent care for his people in difficult days—there is great meaning in such passages. Literalized, they lead traditionalists of the twentieth century to conjuring up strange applications to our time, and give rise to a premillenarian outlook which is more rooted in hopelessness than hope.

The fourth type, which blends external with internal history, is the most numerous in the Bible, and the most crucial. Hebrew history, together with the historical sections of the New Testament, has more than a few examples of this blending of history with story. The most important are the stories of the birth and resurrection of Jesus, with the intervening miracles.

To say that these stories are not true is to court dismay from those to whom they are precious. They are too true to be discarded; too much hinges on them. But true *in what way?*

The best answer, I would say, is that they represent a combination of historical fact with the distilled essence of loving, grateful memory which has given them not only fragrance but profound meaning. Sad, indeed, would be the day when we dropped the Christmas and Easter stories from our Christian faith and life. These things happened! Jesus Christ is our living Lord because they happened! But just *how* they happened we do not know, nor do we need to know in objective, scientific terms.

If I understand Professor Bultmann, it is this meaning and power that he thinks can best be preserved for a scientifically oriented generation if myth is seen as myth rather than as history. With this design I feel much sympathy, but would diverge at two points. First, I believe that the main events (not in every detail) in the life, ministry, death, and resurrection of Jesus are not only accessible to us but indispensable. Second, we can discard the spatial cosmology of a three-story universe, as most moderns do, but we cannot so easily part with the time sense embedded in the biblical view of history. In short, we can put question marks after many of the miracle stories and other difficult passages, but we cannot discern the message of the Bible unless we see in it the forward-pointing, hope-renewing purposes of God.

These purposes are discerned through our experience, as, of course, everything else we know comes to us in some way through experience. Yet our experience does not generate them; it transmits them. These purposes are the purposes of God, not of ourselves, and they are made known to us through what God has done, objectively, in history. Those who, like Bishop Robinson,[6] reject a God "out there" as well as "up there" need to be very careful lest they place God within us instead of seeing him as "the high and lofty One that inhabiteth eternity," the God who has come to us within history in Jesus Christ.

4. History and the covenant

We shall close this chapter with some observations on the central note in the biblical view of history, God's covenant with his people, and its bearing on our situation in today's world.

The biblical narrative places the institution of God's covenant with his people in the time of Abraham (Gen. 17:1-8) with a still more general covenant in his promise to Noah (Gen. 9:8-17). We are probably on firmer ground to say that it began with Israel's emergence to nationhood under Moses, but the time of its beginning is not crucial to its meaning.

The primary notes in Israel's faith are the union in their God of sovereign power with righteousness, and also a union of the righteousness which demands obedience with mercy and steadfast love even in the midst of judgment. All these notes are found in the covenant relation. It was not an evenhanded, two-sided bargain between equals; it was on God's side a covenant of grace

---

[6] Cf. *Honest to God,* especially Chapter I.

which demanded obedience, and on man's part the covenant called for response to this grace in loyal obedience and with faith in God's eternal faithfulness.

This is directly related to the biblical view of history. Most obviously, it is related in the fact that the covenant was repeatedly violated in the course of Israel's history, and the prophets had again and again to call the people back to fidelity by proclaiming both the judgment and the redemptive mercy of God. It is related in its foundations as well as its fruits, and in a way which combines external and internal history. Both the events of Hebrew history and the interpretation the people placed upon them—notably but not exclusively the exodus from Egypt and the giving of the covenant on Sinai, then Israel's conquest of Canaan, her struggle with her foes, and finally the exile and return—are impregnated with the idea that the supreme Ruler of heaven and earth had in a special way chosen Israel as his people and was concerned in all their fortunes. It was not a covenant of merit, for it was never assumed that Israel deserved to be thus chosen; it was a covenant of grace.

In some respects the morality of Israel follows the common pattern of primitive societies; in others the morality of the covenant and its embodiment in reverence for the law, divinely ordained, is unique among Israel's contemporaries. It centers in the event and the promise which the nation in her worst days never entirely forgot:

You have seen what I did to the Egyptians, and how I bore you on eagles' wings and brought you to myself. Now therefore, if you will obey my voice and keep my covenant, you shall be my own possession among all peoples; for all the earth is mine, and you shall be to me a kingdom of priests and a holy nation (Exod. 19:4-6).

Then came Jeremiah with this announcement of the new covenant, written in the hearts of men (Jer. 31:31-34), and its fulfillment in the coming of Christ. Stemming from the Second Isaiah's grasp of the universality of God's love, and made manifest in history through the mission to which Jesus felt God had called him, the covenant which had centered in God's relation to his chosen people now reached out to embrace all mankind. And the church, the New Israel, was God's chosen agent for its extension. There is a striking similarity, yet a new and deeper note, in I Pet. 2:9-10 compared with the passage quoted above from Exodus.

But you are a chosen race, a royal priesthood, a holy nation, God's own people, that you may declare the wonderful deeds of him who called you out of darkness into his marvelous light. Once you were no people but now you are God's people; once you had not received mercy but now you have received mercy.

In our time we find ourselves in a curious paradox. We shrink from the whole idea of a "chosen people." It seems like an unjust kind of favoritism, and the projection of a collective egotism on the part of a people or its leaders. At the same time, whether we admit it or not, we tend to think of our country as "God's country," and our nation as being in a special way the recipient of God's favor.

As Christians we cannot in any literal sense return to the Old Testament idea of a chosen people and covenant community. The New Testament, which very significantly means the New Covenant, carries us to a wider outreach with a commission which echoes but transcends the call of the Second Isaiah to Israel to become a "light to the Gentiles." Yet only at great loss does the church disregard the deep meaning of the covenant in its attempt to find its place in today's world.

This meaning is centered in the nature of the covenant God. The "Ground of being" he is, and the "Unconditioned." Yet I cannot think that this is enough. The God of Christian faith is the Creator of heaven and earth, the Sovereign Ruler of nature and history, the righteous Judge of all men including ourselves, the Source of all goodness and supremely of redemptive love. To such a God we can pray, and expect to receive from him guidance, comfort, and strength. With such a God, both as individuals and as a church, we can enter into a covenant of loyal obedience.

With power comes responsibility, and America is in a sense a "chosen people" because of its immense power among the nations of the world which entails extraordinary obligations. The day has passed for the United States and the newer democracies when the activities of church and state can be blended as they were in theocratic Israel. Yet the word of the psalmist has not been superseded, and never can be.

Blessed is the nation whose God is the Lord,
    the people whom he has chosen as his heritage! (Ps. 33:12.)

What might extricate us from the dilemma of being and not being a chosen people, and at the same time induce in us a deeper humility, a more firmly grounded hope, and a wider outreach in service, would be a more "existential" recognition of our relation to the covenant God. It is easy to say in a sentence that in God are united sovereign power, an insistent righteousness, and redemptive love. It is not so easy to organize our total living as if we believed it to be true.

I was about to say that these truths are proclaimed from many pulpits every Sunday. Yet I am not so sure that they are, at least in the sense that they become *kerygma,* the life-transforming and life-invigorating gospel that they ought to be. If they were, America might more truly be "this nation under God."

Faith in the God of the covenant is, of course, not all that is needed for the well-being of our nation and the world today. A great deal of political action and economic readjustment is necessary, particularly in ensuring basic human rights, and in reducing the great disparities of economic and social privilege by helping the underprivileged to help themselves. Yet without such faith in God, the motivation for such action will be greatly enfeebled.

I propose to end this chapter with two quotations, the one majestic poetry, the other a simple bit of rhyme. In both, I believe, are stated authentic grounds of hope in the God whose everlasting covenant still holds fast today.

The first is from the Seventy-fifth Psalm. Significantly, it is introduced with the words, "To the choirmaster," and the tune is indicated, which suggests that it was meant to be sung as a paean of hope and confidence. Let us listen to it in the Moffatt translation.

> We offer thanks to thee, O God, we offer thanks to thee,
> telling of all thy wondrous deeds.
> God says, "Through all the long delay
> I am still ruling in my justice;
> when men in any panic melt away,
> I still uphold the order of the world." (vss. 1-3.)

Taken seriously, what these words signify could do more than the most artful human devices to "uphold the order of the world" amid the deep uneasiness of our times.

The other passage, in complete lack of literary embellishment, says what we have to do about it.

I grew up in a little rural hamlet in northeastern New York, where we had church and Sunday school in a schoolhouse because there was then no church building—and nobody thought much about the separation of church and state. We sang innumerable times No. 147 in the little gospel songbook that was used, and its refrain went like this:

> Trust and obey,
> For there's no other way
> To be happy in Jesus,
> But to trust and obey.[7]

I do not commend this as great poetry, or its rhythm as great music. Yet it is profoundly true, and it is this message which comes to my mind now across the decades, for it is also the word of our covenant God from across the centuries.

---

[7] John H. Sammis, "When we walk with the Lord."

V

THE KINGDOM

OF GOD

We come now to a theme very intimately related to that of the previous chapter, and indeed to that of the entire book. So central, yet so far-reaching and so open to various interpretations, is the concept of the kingdom that it has seemed best to devote a chapter entirely to it instead of trying to touch it tangentially at the many points where it is relevant.

Accordingly, that the reader may get a picture of how vital, yet how controversial, is the subject of the kingdom, we shall begin with a rapid survey of its status in contemporary thought. Then, in the attempt to weave these threads together and distinguish truth from error as the author sees it, we shall examine the biblical bases of the concept. Although the explicit references to the kingdom appear much more often in the New Testament than the Old, we must look at its rootage there. Central attention, however, must be given to the words of Jesus on the kingdom. The last section, as in previous chapters, will take note of its bearing on Christian hope amid the distressing situations of the world today.

1. Points of agreement

There are certain elements in the Christian understanding of the kingdom about which there is general agreement, and these had better be stated first as a platform to stand on while we look at the disagreements.

First, *the kingdom means the sovereign, righteous rule of God.*
It is a rule in which power and goodness, judgment and mercy,
are combined, as was noted in relation to the covenant. Though
the term arose at a time when nations were monarchies, and it
had, perhaps, a more realistic symbolism before political democracies became the order of the day, it connotes power exercised in loving concern rather than in arbitrary dictatorship.
Jesus' understanding of God was of one whose power is kingly
but whose love is that of a father.

Second, *this sovereign rule of God must be accepted by men in
faithful, grateful obedience.* There is no kingdom without subjects. The kingdom is not destroyed by men's disobedience, for
God still rules in judgment. Yet the summons to "seek first his
kingdom and his righteousness" entails human response. This, I
believe, would be agreed to even by those who contend most
vigorously that it is God's action, not man's, which brings the
kingdom to fulfillment.

Third, *the goal of the kingdom is a redeemed society.* Note that
I did not say a "reconstructed social order." About this there is
much disagreement. By redeemed society I mean: (1) that the
kingdom is inextricably related to salvation; and (2) that it is not
a purely individualistic, but an individual-in-community, concept.
In short, one does not enter the kingdom of heaven alone, whether
in this life or the next.

Fourth, *the kingdom meets opposition at every point.* This opposition may be spoken of as coming from Satan, or from the
demonic powers of human history, or simply from man's inveterate sin, ignorance, and error. Opinions differ as to whether
to take the opposition of the devil and the demonic as symbolic
or as literal descriptions. Yet no one doubts that the reign of God
in human history meets constant and powerful opposition.

Fifth, *the kingdom points forward.* "Thy kingdom come." The fulfillment of this prayer may be expected on earth and within history, or only beyond the life of man on earth, or in both spheres. Yet the kingdom is not fully present now. Its consummation lies in the future. It is a dynamic hope, not a static achievement.

Finally and basically, *in the kingdom of God lies our ultimate hope.* This is true whether the hope is located on earth or in heaven, whether it is blended with or kept dissociated from the hope of eternal life for the individual. This concept of the kingdom as our ultimate hope is consistent with the fact that the message of the kingdom is the central note in the recorded words of Jesus. While there is nothing in New Testament interpretation and scarcely anything in Christian theology in which there is less unanimity as to how to think of it, nobody doubts its close relation to Christian hope.

2. Varieties of understanding

For centuries the primary understanding of the kingdom was in terms of individual salvation. One entered the kingdom when he was converted or was baptized into membership through the agency of the church, and could therefore look forward to the blessedness of heaven after death. Undoubtedly, Jesus' use of the "kingdom of God" and the "kingdom of heaven" as synomyms furthered this interpretation. The stress laid by Roman Catholicism on sacramental grace as essential to salvation beyond death, and the otherworldliness of much of pre–twentieth-century Protestantism, contributed to it. As a result, even today the run-of-the-mill layman, though he has a dim idea of the kingdom, thinks of "being saved" quite explicitly as being assured of heaven. If one doubts this, try to discuss salvation with an ordinary church group, and note how soon the questions point in this direction.

A smaller number, though in the totality of the Pentecostal and Adventist groups a large number, have united this emphasis on individual salvation with a millennial hope. Here there is a much more explicit concept of the kingdom. It is based in part on the references to Christ's second coming in the Gospels and Epistles, but given concreteness by the vivid imagery of the book of Revelation, especially Chapter XX.

The heart of the millennial hope is of a blessed interval of a thousand years in which Christ will reign. The premillennialists place Christ's bodily return at the beginning of this millennium. With the earth in a hopeless state, Christ will return and reign with the saints for a thousand years. During this period Satan will be locked up, and the righteous raised. At the end of this time Satan will be unbound for a season and the lost souls raised, only to be condemned to an eternal hell. The earth, then cleansed by fire, becomes the dwelling place of the redeemed. Postmillennialists, interpreting this cryptic chapter somewhat differently, place Christ's return at the end of the millennium, during which time he reigns from heaven. At his return, the great battle of Armageddon is fought, after which comes a general resurrection and final judgment. The earth is destroyed by fire, and a new heaven and a new earth take its place. Thus the two views differ not only in the time of Christ's return but on whether the kingdom comes in a transfigured earth or a realm beyond it.

It is apparent that such millenarianism, whichever type is held to, holds out a lively hope to its adherents. But it is hope only for the righteous few, and portrays a state of hopelessness not only for the remainder but for the world as a whole within the sphere of history. It illustrates both the consequences of taking symbolic language literally and the disparities that ensue even from this procedure.

Unsatisfied with an individualistic and otherworldly idea of salvation within the kingdom of heaven, unable through historical and literary study of the Bible to accept either form of millennialist literalism, liberal theology gave a radically new emphasis to the kingdom. This has been somewhat indicated in Chapter II. The social gospel that was associated with it was in part a product of the evolutionary optimism current in the late nineteenth and early twentieth centuries, with its gradualism reinforced by the parables of the mustard seed and the leaven (Matt. 13:31-33; Luke 13:18-20). Yet only in part. It was due far more to an awakened conviction that God requires of his servants and subjects in the kingdom a cleansing of the earth, not by fire, but by deeds of mercy and justice. Since the shackles that bound men to a kingdom of evil (a term prominent in the thought of Walter Rauschenbusch) were not alone personal sins but great, unjust social institutions, these must be attacked with a sense of divine urgency. Hence, the mandate of God for men to devote themselves to "building the kingdom."

The inadequacy of this view has already been suggested. Not only was it often too optimistic and utopian, but it tended to center too much in the activity of man rather than the regnancy of God. The social gospel cannot be identified with the kingdom, and few if any theologians today attempt thus to identify it. Yet the exponents of this position within the churches were never so utopian and man-centered as its critics of today are prone to assume. Furthermore, its challenge to the evils of society in the name of God and for the love of men was right, and fully consistent with the goals of the kingdom. It is a great pity that this challenge seems considerably to have dropped out of sight in recent years in spite of attempts to maintain it under other theological rubrics.

In the middle 1930's a new interpretation of the kingdom, called "realized eschatology," came upon the scene. It was inaugurated by C. H. Dodd of Cambridge University and set forth in his *The Parables of the Kingdom* and other writings. Its central note is that in the coming of Jesus Christ the kingdom came; the *eschaton* entered history. The prophets of the Old Testament had looked for a coming "day of the Lord," that is, the fulfillment of the divine purposes within history, and the apocalyptic writers had envisioned this as a dramatic divine intervention which would bring an end to earthly history. Professor Dodd holds that early Christianity, under the influence of the teachings of Jesus himself, made a profound change in this view. Like Judaism, it rejected recurrent cycles of history, and looked back to a real beginning and forward to a real end, conceiving the process from beginning to end as directed by the purpose of God. But with a difference. The Lord had come!

Whereas Jewish eschatology looked to the close of the historical process as the necessary fulfilment upon which the meaning of history depends, Christianity found the fulfilment of history in an actual series of events within history—namely the life, death and resurrection of Jesus Christ, and the emergence of the church as the bearer of his Spirit. History, indeed, still goes on, and at long last it will have an ending. But meanwhile, the true *eschaton,* the event in which its meaning is conclusively revealed, has become an object of experience.[1]

While recognizing some disparity in the sayings about the kingdom in the words of Jesus recorded in the Gospels, Professor Dodd believes that this was his central emphasis, and that this

[1] C. H. Dodd, *et al., The Kingdom of God and History* (Chicago: Willett, Clark & Company, 1938), pp. 25-26.

same conviction is expressed in the fundamental thesis of early Christian preaching that prophecy had been fulfilled in the coming of Christ. New Testament scholars vary as the extent to which they accept realized eschatology, but its influence will be discerned as we move to the next development.

At the same time that a social gospel kingdom was declining in general acceptance and realized eschatology was being much discussed, there was a strong revival of apocalyptic eschatology. This was more widely advocated by European continental theologians than elsewhere, but espoused also by some American neo-orthodox leaders. This put the coming of the kingdom at the end of history, with a dim view of the possibility of its presence within history because of human sin and tragedy and the power of giant "demonic" forces of collective evil.

As far as I know this view does not have a commonly accepted name other than the general designation of biblical eschatology, which is also claimed by others, but we shall call it the transcendent apocalyptic view. This may help to distinguish it from millennialist literalism, from which its exponents have wished to be dissociated. Yet the dissociation has not always been clear, for not only is it definitely "otherworldly" as to the sphere of God's final victory, but it makes much use of the apocalyptic passages in the New Testament, including specific references to the second coming of Christ as the termination of earthly history.

Instead of citing particular exponents of this view, it may be of greater interest to trace its influence through the stages by which the main theme of the Evanston Assembly of the World Council of Churches in 1954 was given its theological formulation.

This theme was "Jesus Christ—the Hope of the World." When this theme was chosen by an administrative committee, it was assumed that this was a note on which all Christians could agree, and a much-needed note amid the darkness of the times. An advisory commission of distinguished Christian leaders,[2] most of them theologians, was set up, and they were asked to spell out the meaning of the theme in preparation for the coming assembly. To give plenty of time, the work was begun in the summer of 1951.

It soon became apparent that agreement was by no means easy to come by. The first report was announced as "not the first draft of the document to be submitted to the Assembly, but rather the opening of a conversation," in which it was hoped that individuals and congregations in all member churches would take part. The conversation, at least in the United States, was immediately forthcoming!

As I read this report now, it seems a pity that so much that was good in it was so largely overlooked. It says some very vital things, not only of the grounding of Christian hope in the wider context of Christian faith, but of its relation both to the world situation and to the church situation today. In the ensuing "conversation," however, much of this was bypassed because it so clearly affirmed the second coming of Christ, which most American liberals assumed had been relegated to the Adventist sects. The opening paragraph states, "It is He who is to come at the last in the glory of His Kingdom as judge and savior of the world, to reveal and consummate His victory." Subsequent references repeat this affirmation.

The volume of comment which followed the issuance of the first report was taken seriously. In the second report [3] after the

[2] Originally twenty-five in number, but thirty-two at the end.
[3] See my article, "Progress in Eschatology," in *The Christian Century*, January 14, 1953, for a fuller statement than can be included here.

commission met in 1952, there was a definite attempt to distinguish between biblical eschatology and crude apocalypticism. There was recognition of the presence of the risen Christ in the life of the Christian believer, and of the difference this makes, here and now. There was a dynamic and vital statement of the bearing of the Christian hope on the problems of contemporary society. The influence of realized eschatology appears in a balance between affirmations that "in Christ the new age has already come," and its future consummation when he returns in glory.

Yet the latter note is very definitely retained. The statement is made repeatedly that we are living between the two ages of Christ's first coming and his expected return. In the first chapter, exclusive of biblical citations, there are nearly twenty references to Christ's return or to his final coming in glory. One vivid paragraph of six sentences introduces every sentence with the words, "When he returns." It affirms that when he returns "that will be the resurrection of the dead . . . , the day of inheritance . . . , the final destruction of evil . . . , the restoration of creation's lost harmony . . . , the union of the Church with her Bridegroom . . . , the final judgment and the consummation of history." The document abounds in biblical citations, presented without reference to context. What results is an even more explicit statement than in the first report of an apocalyptic eschatology centered in the second coming, though it is in better balance with the significance of Christ's first coming. His continual coming in the lives of his followers is in more ambiguous status and is subordinate to either the first or second coming as the basis of Christian hope.[4]

[4] An important conference on "The Meaning of Hope in the Bible" was held under World Council auspices at Zetten, Holland, in April 1952. Walter M. Horton, who attended it, commented thus: "Firm faith in Christ's present triumph (realized eschatology) leads to firm assurance of his final coming (*Parousia*), but confusion and dispute arises over the

Then came the third and final report as the result of the commission's meeting in 1953. It is much longer than either of the others, less vividly written, and less controversial. It has a section on "The Kingdom That Now Is," and one on "Having and Hoping," as well as a much longer one on "The Kingdom That Is to Come." While the basic point of view of the previous reports is unchanged, more attention is given to the practical Christian significance of living in the hope of a kingdom that both has come and is to come. In fact, the discussion of the kingdom occupies less than one fourth of the space of the document, the remainder being given to the church and its confrontation of the world. It contains many excellent observations, and it is regrettable that it received so little attention when it finally appeared.

These five views of the kingdom, thus rapidly surveyed, are by no means all that have appeared in Christian history, although on the whole Christians through the centuries have been much less concerned about the kingdom than about either Christ or the church. Its complete omission from the Apostles' Creed and barest mention in the Nicene may help to explain this oversight. Yet there have been other views, among which a half century ago was the "interim ethic" that was associated with Schweitzer's interpretation of Jesus' apocalypticism—that is, the theory that the ethical injunctions of Jesus were designed only for the brief period before his expected return.

These other views we must pass over, for the five that have been looked at are those which are most germane to contemporary thought. These views or their fruits, and these views

---

way that leads from the first to the second. There was a rather sharp difference of opinion between some of our British and some of our Continental participants over the 'continual' coming of Christ, *versus* his 'first' and 'second' comings." *The Ecumenical Review,* July, 1952, pp. 421-22.

either in their simplest form or in combinations, are still with us. As I attempt a little later to state what I regard as the most satisfactory position on this disputed but enormously important matter, the reader will discern traces of them.

3. The kingdom in the Old Testament

The phrase "kingdom of God" does not appear in the Old Testament, as any concordance will indicate. Yet its foundations are deeply embedded there, and it is impossible to understand what it means in the New Testament without taking into account these foundations. It is significant that the most illuminating treatment of this theme which has appeared in recent years, John Bright's *The Kingdom of God*,[5] is by an Old Testament scholar.

The kingdom concept is rooted in the biblical view of history, with its forward-moving stream of events under the rulership of the sovereign, righteous God. Since all history thus moves toward the fulfillment of a divine purpose, it is natural that one or another conception of the end of history—end both as *finish* and as *fulfillment*—should permeate biblical thinking.

The whole conception of the covenant, at least from the Exodus onward, underlies this view. Yet it becomes more explicit and differentiated in Israel's later history. Three movements, in particular, fed into the stream which we find in the New Testament conception of the kingdom. Since they were intertwined without full consistency, they provide biblical authority for various views of the kingdom—the five that have been outlined and others.

These three streams are prophecy, apocalypse, and the law.

---

[5] (Nashville: Abingdon Press, 1953.) It received the Abingdon-Cokesbury Award for that year.

They have a common center, yet they diverge. All that can be done here is to trace the outlines.

All the prophets believed that God was in control of human destiny, though they could not hold him responsible for human sin. It was on this conviction that they could both give utterance to oracles of doom and hold out hope amid Israel's darkest days. It was on this basis also that they could speak of the coming "day of the Lord" which Amos, contrary to popular hopes, described in these terms:

> Is not the day of the Lord darkness and not light,
>   and gloom with no brightness in it? (5:20.)

Yet brightness to light up the gloom does appear, not in the fortunes of the nation which grew steadily worse, but in the rise of the messianic hope. It was the first Isaiah, even before the fall of Jerusalem, who gave utterance to words which still stir in us joy and hope after twenty-seven centuries:

> The people who walked in darkness
>   have seen a great light;
> those who dwelt in a land of deep darkness,
>   on them has light shined (9:2).

Isaiah, statesman that he was, naturally associated this hope with national glory, and he foretold the coming of a messianic prince of the house of David. Yet he was a realist, and saw clearly enough that Israel, having broken her side of the covenant again and again, could hardly expect to return as an entire nation to days of former greatness. Hence, the doctrine of the remnant, in whom this hope was vested and who were to be its custodians.

In Jeremiah's time the plight of the nation was even worse, and the personal plight of the prophet was desperate. But instead of yielding to desperation, he caught a vision of the universal reign

of God in the hearts of men. Jer. 31:31-34 is a high-water mark
of the old covenant, pointing forward to the new. A little later
Ezekiel, after the blow had fallen and the exile had destroyed
any lingering glory of the house of Judah, portrayed an un-
quenchable hope in his dramatic vision of the valley of dry bones
that by the power of God were made to rise up and live again.
(37:1-14.)

Yet it was in the great prophet of the exile, the Second Isaiah,
that the messianic hope, which was at the same time the hope of
the universal reign of God, came to its highest expression. Of the
Suffering Servant, Bright says that "this is a concept quite without
parallel either in the Old Testament or in the thought patterns of
the ancient Orient." [6] It has antecedents in the sacrificial system
and the corporate solidarity of the nation, but they do not explain it. Yet it was this concept that the prophet used to set forth
the destiny and the hope of the people of God, and the mode by
which God was to establish his kingdom.

Do the Servant poems which appear so often in the Second
Isaiah's message [7] predict the coming of Christ? Probably not, as
prediction is commonly understood. Yet they do foretell the consummation of the hopes of Israel. This was not to be the glorious
national restoration they had longed for, but victory through the
triumph of God amid the humiliation, suffering, and defeat of
the Servant. Its price was to heed the call of God to become the
servant of all mankind.

There are differences of opinion as to whether the Servant
means Israel or the promised Messiah. The implications of the
poems swing back and forth. But the prophet was not writing for

[6] *Op. cit.*, p. 148.
[7] Although the lists vary somewhat among biblical scholars, one is on safe
ground to include 42:1-4; 49:1-6; 50:4-9; 52:13–53:12; 61:1-3.

critical scrutiny centuries hence! He was pouring his heart out with a great new conviction of what the Lord of heaven and earth was both promising and demanding of his people. It seems fair to say that the Servant is Israel—not all Israel, but those true to the covenant in loyal obedience—and at the same time One whom God will send to lead the servant people.

So much for the foundations of the kingdom in prophecy. But what of apocalypse?

There are only two apocalyptic books in the Bible, Daniel and Revelation, though there are fragments elsewhere, and there is much apocalypse in the intertestamental writings. This vision literature, with its strange beasts and cryptic numbers, usually appeals to us less than the majestic words of prophecy. Yet because it is unmistakably in the Bible, it has contributed more than a little to modes of understanding the kingdom.

Although the nation's fortunes appeared to pick up somewhat after Cyrus permitted the return from exile in Babylon, these were still very troubled times. In reality there was no nation, only occupied territory under a foreign power. In such a situation it is not surprising that hopelessness—as far as this world goes—succeeded hope. Yet faith did not die; it was too deeply embedded through centuries of trust in the God of the covenant. God *must* surely triumph! His purpose *must* be fulfilled! The hope then became transformed into the expectation of a great, cataclysmic, divine intervention. This old earth could end—no great matter— so long as a new heaven and a new earth ensued in which God would reign and his righteous ones would live with him in glory.

There was far more than hopelessness in such a view. It bred great courage in the face of persecution. The book of Daniel was written during the persecution of the Jews under Antiochus Epiphanes; Revelation, nearly three centuries later when the

Roman emperor Domitian was persecuting the Christians. Both bade their readers to be steadfast, for God was on their side. One of the great passages of the Old Testament is that in which Daniel is represented as saying to King Nebuchadnezzar, "Our God whom we serve is able to deliver us from the burning fiery furnace; and he will deliver us out of your hand. . . . But if not, be it known to you, O king, that we will not serve your gods or worship the golden image which you have set up" (3:17-18).

However, it is in the seventh chapter of Daniel that the passage is found which most directly affected New Testament thought. In spite of Antiochus' pretensions (the beast with the little horn pretending to be great), there sits the Ancient of Days in majesty, able and ready to slay the beast. But this is not all. "Behold, with the clouds of heaven there came one like a son of man," and the Ancient of Days gave to him dominion and power, with the promise that all people, nations, and languages should serve him, and his kingdom should be everlasting (Dan. 7:9-14). It is apparent that Christian thought feels the effects of this passage to the present day.

At this time also arose the custodians of the law, the makers of the Judaism which in Jesus' time was represented by the Pharisees and scribes. Emphasis on the law was not a new thing, for Israel had held it in high esteem from the time of Moses. When it was honored more in the breach than the observance, the prophets had again and again called on the people to observe the requirements of justice and mercy that were embedded in it. But as prophecy declined, the law became externalized; its letter rather than its spirit was accented; a multitude of minute requirements, particularly in matters of sabbath keeping and dietary regulations, was added to it. So complicated did it become that a group of professional interpreters of the law became necessary.

It is a familiar fact that Jesus repudiated such minutiae, and Paul has much to say of the gospel versus the law. It might seem, therefore, that the law has no contributory relation to the kingdom. Yet there is a connection beneath the surface, for the custodians of the law had their hope, too, of a final triumph of the purpose of God within human events. Their idea was that the people of God must become a holy commonwealth. Only by obedience to the law could one be righteous in the sight of God, and only by the righteousness of God's people could the day of the Lord be brought to fulfillment. The vision of the coming of the kingdom was their dream also.

Thus, the prophetic and the legalistic strains have a common center; namely, moral obedience to what God commands. They diverged in New Testament times, as they still do. Yet both took seriously the disciplines of holiness if Israel (or the New Israel of the church) was to find favor in God's sight. The apocalyptic emphasis, on the other hand, was chiefly on waiting in faith and with courage amid danger for God to act. All these emphases persist in the twentieth century.

4. The kingdom in the New Testament

We come now to a crucial part of our survey, the kingdom as it appears in the New Testament, and especially in the recorded words of Jesus. While everybody agrees that this was his central message, we have seen what widely different interpretations emerge from it.

The problem lies in the paradoxes of the kingdom. The words of Jesus can be cited to indicate that it comes gradually or suddenly; in this world or the next; in the response of the individual or in a new society, which in turn may be the fellowship of the church or a larger brotherhood. Though initiated by God, there

are variants as to man's part in bringing it to pass. As we saw
in looking at realized eschatology, there is the question as to
whether Jesus believed that he had inaugurated it by his coming. The apocalyptic interpretation raises the question as to
whether he expected to return to consummate the kingdom by
his own second coming.

There is no likelihood of reaching full agreement. But, at least,
we can understand why the paradoxes are there in the Gospels.

Jesus grew up in an atmosphere saturated with various forms of
hope—all stemming from hope of the coming kingdom through
the fulfillment of God's promise. The nationalist party, led by
the Zealots but embracing others who did not so regard themselves, were looking for a Messiah who would throw off the
Roman yoke and "restore the kingdom to Israel" (Acts 1:6). The
Pharisees expected God to send his Messiah, but not until the
people by obedience to the law had proved themselves worthy
of membership in a holy commonwealth. The apocalyptists were
looking for a Son of Man to come from heaven by divine fiat, as
Daniel had suggested, with a quick end to this earthly regime
and the inauguration of a new one.

And, there in the background, were the teachings of the
prophets about the God of justice and mercy; the time-honored
Shema that was taught to every Jewish boy, "Hear, O Israel; the
Lord our God is one Lord; and you shall love the Lord your
God with all your heart, and with all your soul, and with all
your might" (Deut. 6:4-5); and the word from the Leviticus code,
"You shall love your neighbor as yourself" (Lev. 19:18). All
these, and much more from the Scriptures of his fathers, Jesus
had learned in the carpenter's home and synagogue school of
Nazareth.

It is clear that as Jesus came to maturity and began to announce his message he repudiated completely the hope of the Zealots for a political Messiah and a restored Israelitic nation. He chided the Pharisees for their narrowness and meticulous legalism, but he said that he came not to abolish but to fulfill the law (Matt. 5:17). He felt a deep sympathy with the teaching of the prophets, particularly with that of the one we now call the Second Isaiah, whose words he read as a keynote to his ministry in his first sermon in the Nazareth synagogue:

> The Spirit of the Lord is upon me,
> because he has anointed me to preach good news to the poor.
> He has sent me to proclaim release to the captives
> and recovering of sight to the blind,
> to set at liberty those who are oppressed,
> to proclaim the acceptable year of the Lord (Luke 4:18-19.)

So far, there is little disagreement. About two other matters directly related to the kingdom there are large differences of opinion. One is whether Jesus believed himself to be the promised Messiah, thus fulfilling his people's hopes and inaugurating the kingdom by his coming, and the other is what to do with the numerous apocalyptic passages ascribed to him in the Gospels.

I can claim no definitive wisdom in the matter, but can only give the reader my own opinion. As to the first, Jesus seems to have regarded himself as standing within the prophetic tradition, and in particular, to have been called of God to carry forward the mission of the Suffering Servant announced in the book of Isaiah. This, we noted, was unique. It had largely been lost sight of in the intervening years, but Jesus recovered it in a unique embodiment of his message with his mission, of his life and ministry with his death and resurrection. We are justified, from our side, in saying that he *was* the Messiah—or the Christ, the anointed one, as Christians prefer to call him. Whether he thought of himself in that light we do not know. Since there are passages which point in either direction, the evidence is divided.

As to the apocalyptic question, possibly some of the passages represent the thought of the early church and were interpolated into the Gospels. Possibly some words spoken by Jesus to predict the coming destruction of Jerusalem, so poignantly anticipated in Luke 19:41-44, were taken to refer to the end of the world.[8] Perhaps other words anticipating his own resurrection were taken to mean that he would soon return in a second coming. Yet when due allowance is made for possibilities, there is too much apocalypticism left in the Synoptic Gospels to dispose of the question.

It seems truer to the total record to say that probably Jesus did in some measure accept the apocalyptic expectations of his day. With so much of it all around him, it would not be surprising if he did. Yet with a sure insight he transformed it. No longer, in his outlook, was it pessimistic and hopeless about this world, or a spectacular cataclysm for which man could do nothing but wait. To be sure, it was God who would bring it to pass—and no man by saying "lo, it is here!" or "there!" could calculate the time of the kingdom's coming. What men could do was to "seek first his [God's] kingdom and his righteousness," prize it above all earthly goods, and find their place in it through humble service to their fellowmen. The blending of apocalypse with the highest spiritual and moral insight is epitomized in the parable of the Last Judgment in Matt. 25, where one's place in the kingdom, in the words of the King, is to be determined by deeds of mercy and brotherhood: "Truly, I say to you, as you did it to one of the least of these my brethren, you did it to me" (vs. 40).

[8] Cf. Dodd, *The Parables of the Kingdom* (New York: Charles Scribner's Sons, 1961), pp. 60 ff.

5. Its meaning for our time

It is fortunate that Christians can unite in a great loyalty to God as he has come to us in Christ, and can engage together in works of faith, hope, and love, without full agreement as to the nature of the kingdom. Otherwise we should be in a more sorry state of disunity than that in which our denominations now place us.

As indicated in regard to Jesus' messiahship and his apocalypticism, I have no final answer. Yet I have some convictions, and these have some affinity with all five of the positions previously outlined without being a replica of any of them. As I state what I believe to be the basic notes in the kingdom, I shall at the same time suggest its relevance to contemporary life. The most essential things which Jesus said about the kingdom are not for his time only, but for all times.

It seems clear that Jesus directed his message primarily to individual lives rather han to social structures, though he never thought of the individual in isolation from those about him. Jesus was not trying to be a systematic theologian, neatly defining the nature of the kingdom, and it need not trouble us that there are some inconsistencies in his words. What he did do, unequivocally and with great forcefulness, was to set forth the conditions of entrance into God's kingdom. These conditions, announced in parable after parable, are the need of childlike trust, eager quest for God and devotion to God's call at all costs, humility, sincerity, steadfastness, watchfulness, and fidelity in the stewardship of God's gifts. In short, the faithful service to God in the manifold circumstances of life.

Such living is enormously important today. And it is to be seen in the lives of persons, ordinary persons in whom are seen an extraordinary Christian devotion. Together they make up a great company that no man can number, and in them the kingdom is *here.*

As was indicated at the end of both the first and second chapters, the hope of life after death for the Christian individual is enormously important. I do not, therefore, feel like branding the "otherworldliness" of exponents of individual salvation as escapist. Yet the proper fulcrum of the position that identifies entering the kingdom with becoming a Christian believer is for the present life, with a confident trust that our destiny in the next is in God's hands.

I find less to challenge me in the millennialist position, and reject most of its assumptions. I do not believe that we are living in the last days, unless nuclear destruction, which can hardly be the will of God, precipitates the *eschaton.* I do not believe that Christ will return through the clouds, nor do I believe in any second coming except in a symbolic sense. (Of this, more later.) Yet I have lived in the Orient, where the Pentecostals go everywhere to give their witness, and I cannot but admire their evangelistic zeal which is often linked with medical care and other social services. I wish that all the churches with a better theology had as much concern to witness to their faith.

I have long believed in both the legitimacy and the necessity of a Christian social gospel, and I still do. It is imperative if either the prophets' summons to justice in human society or Jesus' embodiment of the law in the two great commandments is to be fulfilled. I do not think I was ever a utopian as to the prospects of the full consummation of the kingdom hope on earth, and certainly am not now. Yet that this hope at one time seemed less fantastic than it now seems is evidenced by a hymn still found in some of our hymnals:

> At length there dawns the glorious day
> By prophets long foretold;
> At length the chorus clearer grows
> That shepherds heard of old.
> The day of dawning brotherhood
> Breaks on our eager eyes,
> And human hatreds flee before
> The radiant eastern skies.

The author of this hymn, Ozora S. Davis, was a valiant social prophet who died before experiencing either the fulfillment of the hopes thus expressed or the scorn of other men at his deep-rooted Christian optimism.

Yet there is a sense in which a hymn like this states a truth more profound than appears in any easy rejection of the coming of the kingdom through the dawn of brotherhood. In Chapter III, I cited numerous evidences of a forward movement in human affairs. If this trend is understood not in terms of evolutionary optimism or a secularized trust in human engineering, but as a part of the way in which God is working out his purpose in human destiny, it is not inappropriate to see in it the gradual coming of the kingdom. The parables of the leaven and the mustard seed *are* in the Bible! But it takes man's obedient cooperation— a great deal of it—to battle human evil enough to move even a little way toward the fulfillment of God's design.

Realized eschatology has focused fresh attention on an old truth; namely, that the coming of Jesus marks a new epoch in human affairs. His coming to reveal God's purpose for mankind was the most decisive event in human history. It is the center of history in a far deeper sense than the fact that we date our chronology from the reputed date of his birth. But did Jesus himself announce that in him the kingdom had come? I do not so, read the relevant passages. Such affirmations as "the time is ful-filled, and the kingdom of God is at hand" (Mark 1:15), and "the kingdom of God is in the midst of you" (Luke 17:21), are at least equally open to the interpretation that the power of God which was to bring the kingdom to fulfillment was already at work in their midst. In this sense, it is still at work, and it is the ground of our Christian hope.

I suggested earlier the possibility of taking the second coming as symbolic of a final consummation. In this sense, if it is clear that New Testament apocalypticism is not translated wholesale into the present scene, one may tentatively go along with it. I know of nothing in the Bible that so much needs to be "demy-thologized." It is understandable that those who went through the crucible of persecution and grave danger in the struggle against Nazism should find their hearts lifted to new heights of hope and courage by it. Nevertheless, I do not believe that its mythological language ought, even by implication, to be made basic to our understanding of the ultimate fulfillment of God's purpose for humanity. When this is done, even though adequate stress on Christ's first coming may be retained, the emphasis is almost inevitably shunted away from the present scene. It is our risen Lord's continuous coming as Holy Spirit to those who will accept his peace and heed his call to service that is our most vital ground of hope.

I do believe that God's kingdom, already present in foretaste, is coming in fullness in a realm beyond earth and history. The stir-ring words of the "Hallelujah Chorus," with its "He shall reign forever and ever!" never fail to move me. But if we are to be lifted by this hope, we must not only keep on praying "Thy king-dom come," but we must pray and labor faithfully that God's will be done on earth as it is in heaven.

VI

"IF A

MAN DIE"

THIS QUESTION OF JOB'S, "IF A MAN DIE, SHALL HE LIVE again?" has been asked for many centuries, and it is asked today. Without an affirmative answer, Christian hope, though it need not be wholly surrendered, is greatly truncated and foreshortened.

Throughout the greater part of Christian history, and indeed throughout the history of most of the world's religions, the question did not need to be often asked, for an affirmative answer was the accepted belief. Today this answer can no longer be taken for granted. Yet men and women, and choice young people just coming to maturity, and lovely little children keep on dying— always with great grief to those who love them, and often with a great unanswered question in the hearts of those who are left. If Christian hope is to reach life's depths, the answer must not be evaded.

Yet it too often is evaded, sometimes in the most surprising places. Reference was made in the previous chapter to the advisory commission's report on the main theme, "Jesus Christ— the Hope of the World," in preparation for the Evanston Assembly of the World Council of Churches in 1954. Many words appear in it on the kingdom of God, the church, and the encounter of the Christian gospel with the prevailing ideologies of our time. Yet almost nothing on the Christian's personal hope of eternal life! By careful combing I found it mentioned: "And we hope also for our own participation in the endless life of His Kingdom. Of that participation we possess a sure token in His power to make our bodies the temple of His Spirit and to raise us from our daily dying." [1]

True enough. But with this brief reference the document goes on immediately to speak of the church as the body of Christ, of its relation to earthly communities, and of the cosmic transformation of all creation. These are brought together in the sentence, "Christ our hope thus embodies in Himself the destiny of individuals, of the Church, of earthly communities, and of all creation." The personal destiny of the individual gets into the report by the "narrow door" which it says Christians are summoned to enter in their living, but in view of its paramount importance to these same individuals it is strange that not more is said of it.

1. Changing patterns of thought

This overshadowing and near-omission is typical of changes which have come over both popular and theological thought in the twentieth century. The changes have taken somewhat different currents in these two areas, although there is a relation between them. Let us begin with the former.

For forty centuries of recorded history, and probably much longer, man has stubbornly refused to believe that death ends everything. Whether the life after death was conceived as a scene in which the ruler must be served with all the accouterments of power; or as the plain man's passage to the happy hunting grounds; or as union with Brahma, the great oversoul; or a linkage of spirit with ancestral tablet; or transmigration of the soul into another body; or a journey across the Styx to the Elysian

---

[1] "Christ—the Hope of the World." Documents on the Main Theme of the Second Assembly, Section I, E.

fields; or a shadowy life in Sheol; or a voluptuous paradise; or immortal life in our Father's house of many mansions, a deeply embedded faith in personal existence beyond death has persisted. Not only has it affected burial customs, which have produced artifacts indicative of cultures, and adorned the poetry and legends of every people, but we may well believe it has given hope and comfort to bereaved survivors on innumerable occasions.

At present such ideas are neither wholly abandoned nor warmly espoused. They are, of course, dismissed in communist ideology as superstitious notions. Many outside of the communist orbit have strong suspicions that the traditional affirmation of life after death is as much a cultic vestige of an earlier day as are the Elysian fields of classical Greece. Yet even where other aspects of an inherited religious faith are feeble, the light of hope refuses wholly to be extinguished. Buddhism in Japan is at its strongest in burial rites and the honors due to one's dead but somehow living ancestors; the Christian even marginally related to the church wants a religious service with its great promises and words of comfort when death invades his home.

There are no statistics, and none are procurable, by which to know to what extent the American people hold to a vibrant and sustaining faith in eternal life. Large numbers in the churches and synagogues certainly do, with probably less doubt of it in Roman Catholicism than elsewhere. When President Kennedy was struck down by an assassin's bullet, many thousands of all faiths went not only to the rotunda of the Capitol to pay their tribute to a beloved leader, but to their churches for spiritual strength. "In helplessness and despair we fell back on faith in God, noting gratefully how often the late President had been so sustained. . . . All over America people flocked to their churches. Never had divine worship meant so much to so many. . . . Our people drew mightily upon the spiritual resources which are always ours to take if we but seek them in penitence and faith." [2] This does not guarantee that all who went to churches on that fateful weekend, or all who followed with deep solemnity on their television sets the Pontifical High Mass of President Kennedy's funeral, believed with their minds in personal immortality. However, it does indicate with striking clarity the deep, under-the-surface connection between death and religious faith.

Yet life goes on, commonly on the surface in a lighter vein, too often beneath the surface in darker moods unilluminated by such high moments of faith. Where this occurs, belief in personal life after death or in any kind of destiny beyond the earthly scene is often doubted or rejected outright. Why does this occur?

A factor which is both cause and effect is the general uncertainty, confusion, and aimlessness of the times. While not all persons are caught in the prevailing anxiety, dread, and frustration which add up to a sense of life's meaninglessness, many are. Many others who would say with their lips that they believe in God, affirming with their minds a concept which is part of our cultural inheritance, feel no personal relation to God, and their lives go on as if God did not exist. The inevitable pains and problems of existence are then more likely to evoke cynicism, or at best a stoical fortitude, than either faith or hope. Death adds not only to the mystery but to the misery of existence. Where this state of mind prevails, which a firm faith in eternal life as part of the overarching purposes of God could go far to dispel, such rebellion and hopelessness tend further to undercut the grounds of eternal as well as temporal hope.

When this happens, people look elsewhere for support when

[2] "Apocalypse and After," *The Christian Century,* December 4, 1963, p. 1487.

death invades the circle of those loved. A minister, priest, or
rabbi, out of deference to a custom which outlasts its rootage, is
usually asked to conduct a funeral or memorial service. Yet it is
often from the undertaker and from friends, not from the con-
solations of religion with its affirmations of eternal life, that comfort if any is derived. The designation of the mortician, whether
in compliment or in sarcasm, as a "grief therapist" is tacit recognition that he aims to do—for a sizable consideration—what the
minister cannot do because in the bereaved there is no longer
receptivity to his ministry. This is epitomized in a full-page ad-
vertisement of metal burial vaults in a national magazine under
the caption, "A man you lean on in your lonely hour (your
funeral director)." [3]

Such personal and "existential" abandonment of faith in eternal
life is more potent and probably more widespread than intellectual rejection. It cannot be corrected by argument, for it is seldom
induced by reasoned considerations. Only the demonstration of
Christian love in action, which can lead to reliance not only on
the Christian who shows such understanding love but on the
Christian's God, can touch it. That even the pain of death and
separation can produce an openness of spirit which can lead to
new life in the Spirit is one of the great challenges of our faith,
to be accepted in humble fidelity but never presumed upon.

Nevertheless, quite apart from any personal crisis, there are
those who, on what they regard as impregnable scientific grounds,
have rejected belief in personal existence beyond death.

Of the grounds assumed to be fixed scientific barriers, the most
influential is a type of psychology which leaves immortality no
foundation. If what is popularly called soul or spirit is body only,
or solely the functioning of the neural mechanism and glandular

[3] *Good Housekeeping*, December, 1963, p. 213.

equipment of the body, then it is obvious that when the body dies personal existence must cease. Even when the type of psychology held to makes some place for the existence and freedom of decision of the human spirit, some would say that its indispensable connection with a living human body makes personal immortality impossible.

A second factor is the scientific rejection of biblical cosmology, so closely tied in with traditional views of heaven and hell as the abodes of departed spirits. Since the time of Copernicus four centuries ago, men have known that there is no spatial heaven up in the sky, and that "up" is a variable term depending on what time of day it is. Many an adult has known these simple astronomical facts, yet has gone on putting his heaven in the sky and teaching this to his children for want of anything better to say when death enters the family circle. The coming of the space age makes this the more difficult. Likewise, no informed person now believes that hell is somewhere down beneath the earth's crust. Molten lava, yes, which occasionally erupts from volcanoes with great destructiveness, but hardly a biblical "lake of fire."

Science is not the only consideration leading to changing patterns of popular thought. On moral and religious grounds, many Christians believe that the traditional hell is inconsistent with the love of God as this is incarnate in and taught by Jesus. Heaven is easier to hold to; but as we shall see before this chapter is finished, some reconstruction of thinking in regard to its nature seems imperative.

Outside of the churches and to some extent within them, the mood is so exclusively "this worldly" that our forefathers' attention to the other world either purposely or unconsciously slips out by inattention. Much of this attention to the problems and the demands of love and justice in this world is good. Yet when it is erected into the Christian's sole concern, much that ought not to be lost goes with it.

Finally, there is the waning of those forms of philosophical idealism, whether personalistic or Hegelian, which made the conservation of values in personal existence beyond death an essential part of the understanding of all existence. While philosophy as a whole now gives much more attention to linguistic analysis than to metaphysical problems of any kind, the conservation of values in any but the social scene is among the least of its concerns.

In 1929 I published my first major book, *Conflicts in Religious Thought.* I mention this because its last chapter gives evidence of changing approaches to this persistent problem. It begins with an examination of biological, social, impersonal, and personal immortality to try to indicate why the first three are no immortality at all. It is years since I have heard these seriously defended, though some humanists still call it immortality when they speak of the projection of living beings and their influence into the earthly future. The main part of my chapter presents ten arguments (with the answers!) against personal immortality and eight arguments for it. While there is little, if anything, in the chapter that I do not still believe, I should not put it this way now.

The eight arguments there listed for personal immortality are the reasonableness of the universe, moral optimism, the intrinsic worth of personality, the conservation of values, the problem of pain, man's moral task, the religious experience of humanity, and the character of God. I have no wish to retract any of these. In a proper setting all are relevant and true. Yet the truth that lies in the first seven is centered in the eighth. If men do not find their assurance of immortality in the goodness and power of God, they are not apt to find it elsewhere. And many today do not.

2. Immortality or resurrection?

This brings us to a major change that has come over theological thought as well, though it is of a different nature. I doubt that there are many serious exponents of Christian thought who reject belief in eternal life. Even where little is said of the eternal destiny of the individual, this is presupposed in the belief in the final consummation of the kingdom beyond history. As there is no king without subjects, so there is no kingdom of God, on earth or beyond it, without persons in loving, trustful obedience to the Sovereign of all life. However, one hears little of immortality today in theological circles, except as it is repudiated as a Greek idea imported into Christianity. Instead, the emphasis is on resurrection.

To suggest again this shift in mood by reference to books of an earlier day, Harry Emerson Fosdick in 1913 published *The Assurance of Immortality,* which through the years has been a very helpful popular book on this theme. A third of a century later, in 1945, a distinguished New Testament scholar, Frederick C. Grant, published another excellent book with the arresting title, *Can We Still Believe in Immortality?* His answer was affirmative, but the title indicates that "the acids of modernity," of which Walter Lippmann had written so eloquently in 1929,[4] had eaten considerably into the long-held Christian belief in personal immortality. Were Dr. Grant writing on this theme today, he might need to change the title to *Can We Now Believe in Resurrection?*

[4] In *A Preface to Morals* (New York: The Macmillan Company, 1929).

The famous Ingersoll Lectures on Immortality have continued to be given in King's Chapel, Boston, from year to year, with varying points of view. The lecture for 1955-56 by Oscar Cullmann faces the issue head on with the title *Immortality of the Soul or Resurrection of the Dead?* Here the contrast between the Greek conception of the immortality of the soul and the Christian doctrine of resurrection of the dead is presented with much scriptural evidence. It is a definitive answer to a thoroughgoing Platonism, although in my judgment it does not settle the question as to whether a Christian doctrine of immortality is necessarily Platonic.

There are a number of reasons for this change of focus over the past half century. One is the movement away from philosophical into biblical theology. With this has come the tendency to accent the Hebraic notes in the Bible and to depreciate the Greek elements as foreign interpolations.

A second related reason is apprehension lest immortality be thought of as a natural endowment of the soul apart from the gift of God, and that the soul be conceived as in Platonic thought as a temporary resident within the body. One of the overtones of the dichotomy of body and soul which the resurrection emphasis seeks to correct is the assumption that the body is an evil prison house from which the soul seeks release.

A third factor is the current tendency to regard basic biblical affirmations as symbolic or mythological statements of essential truth. This view is presented effectively in the last chapter of Reinhold Niebuhr's *Beyond Tragedy*. He says that the closing words of the Apostles' Creed were at the time of his graduation from seminary an offense and a stumbling block to young theologians. "Yet some of us have been persuaded to take the stone which we then rejected and make it the head of the corner." [5] He then states that the idea of the resurrection of the body can of course not be literally true. Yet it conveys forcefully in symbolic form the unity of body and soul, the existence of the individual within a society which can hope for a divine transformation, and the meeting point of time and eternity.

The belief in resurrection as contrasted with immortality rests primarily on theological rather than scientific grounds. It is espoused by persons who have often decried liberalism's leaning too far in the direction of capitulation to science. Yet it is the more appealing to many minds because of the convergence of the Hebraic idea of the unity of soul and body with the present psychological assumption of the unity of personality. By viewing death as a complete stop, it avoids the dualism of body and soul implicit in the thought of a deathless soul which lives on after the body dies. Its position is that when death comes an individual's whole being ceases to exist, but by an act of new creation he is given by God a new and heavenly body to be the vehicle of eternal life.

These are weighty considerations. That they affect even the life of prayer, to say nothing of our eternal hope, has been expressed by a theologian known best for his writings on the devotional life. Accenting the difference between the Christian and the Hellenic point of view Charles F. Whiston writes:

Death was for man the total stop and end, not only of his body but also of his spirit. The whole man, conceived in terms of a unity, died. It was therefore required that God should, by a mighty and mysterious act of resurrection, raise not simply a part, but the whole man. . . .

To be aware of this will have consequences upon the mood and

[5] *Beyond Tragedy* (New York: The Macmillan Company, 1937), p. 290.

quality of our relationships with God in praying. Belief that our soul is immortal by nature, apart from God's will, will lead us subtly into feelings of self-sufficiency and self-centeredness, insulated from and independent of God. When we are convinced by and committed to belief in resurrection, we find deepened and strengthened in us the note of utter dependence upon God, issuing in undying thankfulness. It will keep ever before us the note of inescapable divine judgment in our lives.[6]

What shall we make of these considerations? Must we abandon belief in immortality and substitute resurrection as we seek not only to comfort the bereaved but to live stronger Christian lives and to help others to do so?

My judgment is that there is a difference between these two points of view, but that it is a mistake to overaccent the differences. "Eternal life" or "life after death by the power and goodness of God" will apply equally to either view, and this is what is essential. If man were to claim immortality as a natural right, regardless of God, this view would certainly tend to self-sufficiency and self-centeredness, and it would not be Christian. Yet no mature Christian does so. If one does not believe that God is the source of his immortality, he simply gives up believing in immortality.

There is a sharper difference at the point of an implicit dualism of soul and body. It is true that immortality has often been taken by Christians to mean the continuance of a deathless soul separated by death from the body which was its former abiding place. Yet immortality does not have to mean this. If the soul, or spirit, is regarded as essential selfhood, personality, the true being of an individual which exists in this life by the gift of the

[6] From *Teach Us to Pray*, by Charles Francis Whiston. Copyright, 1949, The Pilgrim Press. Used by permission.

Creator and continues by God's gift into the next life under a new mode and vehicle of existence, then immortality is as good a term for this new being as is resurrection.

Resurrection is admittedly the more common biblical term. Yet it is open to doubt that the biblical writers and early creed-makers drew the distinction which we are forced to make between the symbolic and literal meanings of the resurrection of the body. While elsewhere in the New Testament distinctions are drawn between body and soul and between flesh and spirit, it is probable that no such dualism was meant in reference to the resurrection of the dead. It was natural enough to assume that in the resurrection the whole person was raised, since apart from any psychological speculation it seemed that the person *was* his body. This is still the natural assumption prior to analysis. When John Jones's body eats, sleeps, talks, or moves about, *he* does these things; when John Jones's body dies, *he* dies.

It need not surprise us to find this assumption in the Bible, and with it a correlative understanding of resurrection. Yet it may be questioned that the term "resurrection" drawn from this source will bear all the weight which theologians of today tend to place upon it. It meant, indeed, that death is not the last word, for God gives eternal life. This is bedrock for Christian faith. But if we do not "demythologize" the resurrection of the body, we run into the crudest possible conceptions of long-disintegrated physical bodies coming out of their graves by land or sea on the resurrection morning. To illustrate, I remember vividly the evangelist Billy Sunday using all his great powers of pictorial description to portray how on that great Last Day the bodies of sailors long since drowned at sea "will come scrambling up the coral reefs to heaven." For the most part, plain people who never heard the word "demythologize" do in fact demythologize the resurrection of the body today in one way or another. Yet many are simply perplexed or incredulous.

We do well to avoid speaking of "immortality of the soul" with its implied dualism or the equally misleading "resurrection of the body," though I do not suggest tampering with a historic creed. Yet the same objections do not hold for "personal immortality" or "resurrection of the dead." Either of these may be used in a Christian sense.

Nothing more true or stirring has ever been written on this theme than the fifteenth chapter of First Corinthians, where Paul speaks without hesitation of the resurrection of the dead, but also of the distinction between celestial bodies and terrestrial bodies, related as the new wheat to its old kernel, and ends with a triumphant paean of that immortality through God in Christ which gives stability and power to the present life. There are words in the passage, notably verses 51 and 52, which reflect a contemporary expectancy of the end in the immediate future. But these can be passed over in view of the glorious and deathless words which follow:

For this perishable nature must put on the imperishable, and this mortal nature must put on immortality. When the perishable puts on the imperishable, and the mortal puts on immortality, then shall come to pass the saying that is written:

"Death is swallowed up in victory."
"O death, where is thy victory?
O death, where is thy sting?"

The sting of death is sin, and the power of sin is the law. But thanks be to God, who gives us the victory through our Lord Jesus Christ.

Therefore, my beloved brethren, be steadfast, immovable, always abounding in the work of the Lord, knowing that in the Lord your labor is not vain (vss. 53-58.)

These words about immortality are unquestionably in the Bible. There is no question of the correct translation, for the word appears not only in King James but in the Revised Standard Version and the New English Bible. Other affirmations of immortality in reference to man's destiny are to be found in Rom. 2:7 and II Tim. 1:10. While resurrection is the more common biblical term, those Christians who wish to continue to speak of what lies beyond death as immortality have good authority for doing so. So long as personal immortality is not conceived as man's inherent right apart from God's gift, and so long as the soul is not thought of as a phantom something unrelated to either a present earthly or a future spiritual body, immortality is still an authentic term to denote the Christian's hope of eternal life.

3. What is our Christian hope?

We shall leave it to the reader to decide for himself whether he prefers to speak of the assurance of immortality or the resurrection of the dead. As indicated, I believe it is possible to speak of both without inconsistency if each is properly understood in its Christian context. But what of the nature of eternal life? To what may we look forward by the wisdom, the power, and the goodness of God?

Here it behooves us to move with great tentativeness, for "we see in a mirror dimly" (I Cor. 13:12). Paul could say, "What no eye has seen, nor ear heard, nor the heart of man conceived, what God has prepared for those who love him" (I Cor. 2:9-10), God has revealed to us through the Spirit. Yet Paul made no claim to understand all the mysteries of eternity; nor should we. The people of the Corinthian church, like those of our churches today, asked the question, "How are the dead raised? With what kind of body do they come?" (I Cor. 15:35.) Though he did answer it with the glorious song of victory quoted in the last section, his immediate answer was, "You foolish man!"

Yet we are not left in complete darkness. Not only does the Bible give us intimations of the nature of eternity, but if there is enough continuity between the present life and the next to speak of the continuing selfhood of the individual, we may get some intimations of the next life through what we know of God's purposes for us in the present. What we do know or can believe on grounds consistent with the rest of our Christian faith, we should not hesitate to hold to even in the absence of full knowledge.

Our most basic certainty is that after death we shall be in the hands of God, who will provide for us such a mode of existence as is right and good. To him we can trust ourselves and our loved ones without fear. This does not cancel out the pain of separation, but it should alleviate the emptiness and carking anxiety which so often accompany the separation.

This is nowhere in all literature more comfortingly stated than in the words spoken by our Lord to his disciples at their last meeting together: "Let not your hearts be troubled; believe in God, believe also in me. In my Father's house are many rooms; if it were not so, would I have told you that I go to prepare a place for you?" (John 14:1-2.)

Furthermore, though faith in eternal life through the power and goodness of God cannot rest solely on the longings of the human heart, lest it be charged with wishful thinking, nor on the basis of a reasoned philosophy, lest it be subject to finite if not biased thinking, the convergence of hope, reason, and faith ought not to be taken lightly. These come together in the words of Tennyson's "In Memoriam," and perhaps no finer words outside the Bible have ever been written on the life after death:

Thou wilt not leave us in the dust:
Thou madest man, he knows not why;
He thinks he was not made to die;
And thou hast made him: thou art just.

If we believe that this is God's world and that God is good, then there is ample reason to believe that personality is not annihilated with death but that persons, God's supreme and most precious creation, are safe in the hands of God. This does not presuppose the natural goodness of man or give grounds for claiming immortality as an inherent right, but it does put the focus on the love of God, where the biblical witness firmly places it.

A second conviction, presupposed in the first, is that persons here shall be persons there. This does not mean unchanged continuity, but it does imply continuity of selfhood. Certainly without our "terrestrial bodies" there must be new modes and structures of existence. Even if Paul had not spoken of a "spiritual body" in continuity with the old, like a new grain of wheat with its predecessor, we should have known that the new life cannot be exactly like the present. When Paul says that "God gives it a body as he has chosen," this is as fine and probably as accurate a figure of speech as our earthbound minds could devise. If we did not have these words from Paul, we should still have to imagine that God would give us, in our same selfhood, some new vehicle of existence and of communication with him and with one another.

There is, of course, peril in letting the imagination run riot. We must not introduce spatial location and imagery into what must be a nonspatial existence, and this the biblical writers sometimes and many persons to the present have been prone to do. However, there is a greater peril in denying the unique continuity

of the person by denying that there is any life after death, or by
believing in the reincarnation of souls in other bodies on earth,
or by assuming that personal values are somehow conserved in
some vast impersonal reservoir.

If there is such continuity of selfhood, a third certainty as to
the nature of the life after death may be affirmed. This is that
death does not terminate personal fellowship. Above all, our fellowship is with God, and in "God's nearer presence"—a symbolic
but an accurate term in congruence with Christian faith—this
fellowship will be deepened and enriched through loving, grateful
service in ways that God will show us.

But there is precious human fellowship on earth with one another. Must this be ended? Christians often ask wistfully, "Shall
I know my loved ones there?" This query need not be set down
merely to wishful thinking and moral weakness. It is based on a
true intuition that life at its highest and fullest demands fellowship. To this persistent question of the mind and heart we need
not hesitate to answer Yes. A good and loving God has made us
to love one another and has set us in relations of rich fellowship
here; it is irrational to suppose that he abruptly blots out this
fellowship in the larger life. At this point the biblical conception
of the kingdom as communal life has close affinities with the
longings of the heart.

We come now to an issue which is very close to the center of
the question. What is the relation of the individual's present life
to his destiny hereafter?

If there is continuity of the self by the power and goodness of
God—call it immortality or resurrection—it follows that the
choices one makes and the life that is lived on earth are of paramount importance to the next. This is true both of the affirmative

side of the hope of eternal life and the Christian belief in divine judgment.

That eternal life, though it is endless, begins in the present is a primary note of the Gospel of John. It is epitomized in the words, "And this is eternal life, that they know thee the only true God, and Jesus Christ whom thou hast sent" (17:3). It appears repeatedly in the letters of First, Second, and Third John. A similar note is found in Paul's references to dying to sin and being raised with Christ through faith (Col. 2:12; 3:1).

This thought of the presence of eternal life through Christ in the here and now is a very basic note in Christian faith. It is the surest corrective of an escapist otherworldliness. In the Last Supper scene, eternal life is a quality of life that is symbolized by our Lord's washing of the disciples' feet in humble service; by his words about being his friends, loving one another, and keeping his commandments; by his great prayer of self-offering and intercession that all may be one. This is eternal life in the present through commitment to God in Christ, and though we cannot foresee just what form it will take in the life beyond death, we know that our Lord calls us to such living now and forever.

It is important to recognize that eternal life, whether in this life or beyond it, does not mean bare, endless duration. A life going on forever without content would scarcely be one to which anybody could aspire! Nor does it mean timelessness in an abstract sense. While certainly clock or calendar time cannot be imputed to it, this does not preclude either the movement of God toward the consummation of his kingdom or man's succession of rich and joyous experience.[7]

[7] The reader is referred to my final chapter on "Time and Eternity" in *The Providence of God* (Nashville: Abingdon Press, 1960) for further treatment of this subject.

It will not do to describe too pictorially what has traditionally been called heaven. Yet certainly we do not need to eliminate from it the note of joy. Traditional thought has placed this uppermost. Salvation has then been conceived as a life of happiness beyond death. This ought to be kept subordinate to faith in God and fidelity to God, shown in the love of God and one's fellows in this life and the next. Joy is not subordinate because of its unimportance, but because joy is found best through meaningful, loving service.

What of the crown, the harps, the golden streets, and the pearly gates by which heaven has often been symbolized? They are the biblical writers' way of trying to suggest to the imagination what cannot be said in prosaic terms. Of such symbolism Robert J. McCracken has written:

It is all a picture; it is an attempt to express the inexpressible. White robes are symbols of stainless purity, crowns of moral victory, harps of abounding happiness, gold of the timelessness of heaven—gold does not rust—and of the preciousness of it. Stainless purity, moral victory, abounding happiness, infinity—the Easter faith is the promise of something we all want, and never cease to want, something for which our hearts crave, something not to be had in this world, but to be found in heaven.[8]

We are on surer ground regarding these affirmative aspects of eternal life than we can be in reference to the nature of divine judgment. The *reality* of judgment both in time and eternity is certain. Not only does the Bible affirm it repeatedly, but the knowledge of our own sinning and our faith in a God who is not sentimental or nonchalant toward sin substantiates it. Hell is

[8] "Who Wants to Live Forever? An Easter Meditation," *The Churchman*, April, 1958.

manifestly present on earth in the anguished estrangement, rebellion, and bereftness of the sinful and unforgiving, hence unforgiven, human heart, and there is no good reason to doubt that it extends into the afterlife for the sinner who is rebelliously unresponsive to God's proffered grace. As with the figurative language about the crowns, the harps, and the streets of gold, so the fires of hell are the pictorial representations of the utter seriousness of rejecting God.

Here the questions emerge in great profusion. Will there be a great Last Judgment, or does all judgment take place along the way? If the latter, does each person face a special judgment at the moment of death? Will those who have never heard the gospel proclaimed be consigned to hell? Will those "good persons" we know who have loved their fellow men but have not accepted Christ be denied eternal life? Is the door to repentance and acceptance of Christ irrevocably closed by death? What of the old reprobate who, afraid to die, repents on his deathbed? Is he admitted to heaven and the just man rejected? Are those who "die in the Lord" at once made sinless, or must they continue to grow in grace? Do Masses and prayers for the dead avail to change their status? Will all persons eventually respond to God's grace and find joy with him in a universal salvation? Do those who have died have knowledge of loved ones still on this side of the Great Divide? Can there be spirit communication between the living and the dead? And more.

I shall not attempt to answer these questions. I have some opinions, held with varying degrees of tentativeness and certainty. But to state even these opinions, unless it could be in the atmosphere of free discussion and the give-and-take of conversation, would imply greater knowledge than I have. These grave issues are in the hands of God, and in his hands we can safely leave them.

Nevertheless, if we would seek an answer to them, three cautions are in order which may serve as guidelines. First, we must not assume to ourselves the prerogatives of divine wisdom, and on this false assurance of knowledge disparage fellow Christians whose answers may differ. Second, we must not impugn the lovingkindness of a God who loves all his human children, not Christians only. Any conception of divine judgment which is less seasoned with mercy than we humans in our best moments feel is surely unworthy of the "God and Father of our Lord Jesus Christ." Third, we must not minimize the importance of Christian commitment in the present life, for the decisions made here and now and the selfhood thus molded have an inescapable bearing on eternity.

Within this framework we can accept the fact of divine judgment, yet trust that God in his mercy has an eternal destiny for all men and a realm of indescribable blessedness for those who love and serve him best. To be saved by Christ is to find the Way, the Truth, and the Life, now and forever. "Everyone that hath this hope in him purifieth himself, even as he is pure." In this faith we can face the future unafraid.

VII

JESUS CHRIST—THE HOPE
OF THE WORLD

IF THE READER HAS STAYED WITH THE BOOK THUS FAR, it must have become apparent that the author believes profoundly that Jesus Christ *is* the hope of the world. Through him above all other agencies and channels we find God or—to speak more accurately—we are led to that openness of life with ego barriers down whereby God can find us. Christianity is not the only avenue to hope or to strength of character; yet without the message embedded in the words and the ministry, the death, the resurrection, and the living presence of Jesus Christ, neither an individual nor a civilization can have its most buoyant hope or its most enduring strength.

It is appropriate now to examine this conviction with a more direct view than has been possible in previous chapters, where the main themes were the status of man, whether perennial or contemporary, and theologies of history and eschatology most directly related to Christian hope. What will be stated in this chapter has been presupposed throughout. Without this presupposition, the point of view that has been presented would be radically different. Yet it seems appropriate to round out the presentation with a more specific confrontation with him who is "the pioneer and perfecter of our faith."

Everything about the life and teaching, death and resurrection, of our Lord is related to every other aspect. It all hangs together in a great unity. But let us begin with what Jesus taught.

1. "He taught them as one who had authority"

The words quoted as the heading of this section are the editorial comment of the Gospel writers as to the way in which Jesus' contemporaries received his teaching (Matt. 7:29; Mark 1:22; Luke 4:32). Through the words of the New Testament and the long tradition of the church, he is still teaching in many thousands of churches today. Can the same response be indicated?

The answer must be, "Yes—with qualifications." Certainly there is no lack of people to give verbal assent to the greatness, and even to the ultimate authority, of his words. Many of these persons give mental assent as well as verbal, though the number of these is smaller because of the suspicion that what Jesus proclaimed was a beautiful but impractical constellation of ideals ill fitted to this world of woe and strife. Still fewer live either by the searching obligations or the high possibilities embodied in his words when they are taken seriously.

There is considerable disparity in contemporary thought as to whether to turn to the teachings of Jesus to find our basis of Christian hope. To revert to the themes of the last two chapters, there are many who find their hope more largely centered in the coming of the kingdom beyond this earth or in the resurrection beyond the death of the individual. Other contemporary voices emphasize the impossibility of fulfilling the absolute demands of Jesus—a note which, however true, is apt to induce hopelessness rather than hope if it is divorced from the wider context of God's mercy. Yet at the opposite extreme, there is still a good deal of moralistic if not superficial preaching which glosses over the deeper demands of Jesus' words, and is more inclined to accent comfort, peace, and joy than the sterner side of the gospel.

To summarize what Jesus taught is probably superfluous, for it has been done many times, and it is all summed up in the two

great commandments, "You shall love the Lord your God with
all your heart, and with all your soul, and with all your mind. . . .
You shall love your neighbor as yourself" (Matt. 22:37, 39).[1]
Nevertheless, I shall mention briefly the main notes in his teaching with a word in each case as to its bearing on Christian hope,
then suggest its bearing as a whole.

a) The ethical teachings of Jesus are grounded in his own relation to God, and in the relation of worship, love, loyalty, and
glad obedience to God to which he summoned his followers.
God's absolute demands are in complete synthesis with his infinite mercy, grace, and willingness to forgive the penitent sinner
and impart new life. Apart from this relationship, the teachings
of Jesus become simply "counsels of perfection," and inability to
live up to them induces frustration rather than hope. However, to
make this separation is to misunderstand Jesus at the most crucial
point.

b) The central teaching of Jesus in regard to a right relationship to God is embedded in his concept of the kingdom. Since
this has been examined at some length in an earlier chapter, I
shall not repeat what was stated there. It is imperative, however,
that we should not divorce either the demands or the hopes of
the kingdom from life as it is lived in the present and in relation
under God to one another. Jesus never did.

c) Jesus' understanding of God as Father gives him a new
estimate of the worth of every person in the sight of God. Recognition of this worth is today our major ground of hope for a
better society. Not because a person is by nature or achievement
either good or great, but because he is precious to God, he should
be to his fellow men. One comes upon this note on almost every

[1] The reader is referred to my *Christian Ethics*, especially Chapter III,
for a more extensive presentation than can be given here.

page of the Gospels—in the parables of the lost sheep, the lost coin, and the lost boy (Luke 15); in Jesus' plea that "not one of these little ones" should perish or be caused to stumble (Matt. 18:6, 14); in making destiny in the Last Judgment depend on how one has treated "one of the least of these my brethren" (Matt. 25:40); in the assurance that the God who cares for the sparrows and the lilies will care for men (Matt. 6:25-30). As much as Jesus hated sin he could see the hidden worth of the sinner, hence his kindness and reassuring word to the harlot and adulterer (Luke 7:36-50; John 4:7-26). Were there no other words of hope in the Christian gospel, these alone when set in the context of God's love could make a tremendous difference both in the lives of despairing individuals and in a deeply troubled society.

d) With love as the central virtue, the accompanying virtues are those, not of conspicuous physical, political, or economic strength, but of moral integrity and tenderness. The blessed are the humble, the compassionate, the pure in heart, the peace-loving (Matt. 5:3-12). The supreme goal is a determined quest for the way of righteousness in the face of opposition, with unfaltering reliance on the power of God's presence. There is no guarantee of outward security. Yet hope lies at a deeper level, for "blessed are you when men revile you and persecute you and utter all kinds of evil against you falsely" for Christ's sake.

e) Again and again, Jesus says that the way to true greatness is through service. The living of a full, rich, abundant life is, from the human end, to be found through self-forgetful love, even as God has led the way in his self-giving love. "If any man would come after me, let him deny himself and take up his cross and follow me. For whoever would save his life will lose it, and whoever loses his life for my sake will find it." (Matt. 16:24-25.)

"Whoever would be great among you must be your servant, and whoever would be first among you must be slave of all." (Mark 10:43-44.) These are familiar words today, and the greater part of our society professes to believe in the practice of altruism. Nevertheless, much of the prevalent unrest and rebellious feeling of being "put upon" and "given a raw deal" arises from the ego-centric expectation of *receiving* service, and much of it would disappear with a greater eagerness to deny oneself enough to *give* it.

f) Jesus had a great sense of the integral unity of right motive and right fruits as the measure of the moral quality of an attitude or act. He does not balance these against each other in any systematic fashion. Sometimes it is the spirit that prompts the action which is stressed as superior to a legalistic keeping of the commandments; again he points to the rewards, which are to be measured not in man's terms but God's. Both notes appear repeatedly in his teaching and are especially evident in the Beatitudes. Both are essential to a sustaining Christian hope.

g) To come back to our first point, Jesus made unqualified demands. He never watered down God's requirement of righteousness to any easy human achievement. He was apparently not concerned with the moral dilemma posed by the words, "You . . . must be perfect, as your heavenly Father is perfect" (Matt. 5: 48). What he was concerned about was that men should love God supremely, love other men—even one's enemies—as one's self, and seek to live in obedient, trustful relationship to God. His answer to the hard demands of life in the kingdom was not an assurance of human sinlessness, but of new birth by the gift of God.

I have tried to state seriatim what I believe to be the primary notes of both duty and hope in the message of Jesus. However, any analysis loses something of the power that comes from the impact of the message as it comes to us whole. One must go to the Gospels themselves to get the "feel" of it. Within the Gospels it is epitomized most clearly in the Sermon on the Mount.

The Sermon on the Mount may be a collection of sayings assembled from an earlier collection, now lost. Nevertheless, delivered as one discourse or as several, it is the greatest compendium of spiritual and moral wisdom to be found in any literature. If one opens the heart and imagination to its power, it lifts and challenges the soul. It reveals so clearly the personality of Jesus that it has the ring of great authenticity.

A good many years ago a book was published bearing no author's name and entitled simply *By an Unknown Disciple*. The author, apparently preferring anonymity lest a name get in the way of the message, gives an interpretive paraphrase of the gospel story under the guise of being one of the disciples. I can recall reading the Sermon on the Mount from this book to a group of restless students in a college chapel, and seeing their faces turn from playful mischief or boredom to eager response and the stillness of intent listening. It is too long to quote in full, but a paragraph will give its flavor.

God has commanded me that I deliver to you a new Commandment, the law of the Kingdom, love one another. No longer, as in the days of our ancestors, are men to say you must love your neighbour and hate your enemy, for the new Commandment is that you love your enemy also. For if you love only those who love you, what credit is that to you? Do not all outcasts do this? And if you are only kind to them that are kind to you, what thanks do you deserve? That is not God's way. He is kind to the thankless and to the bad. Therefore, I say unto you, you must love your enemies, and show kindness to those who hate you, and if men injure you, you must not seek for revenge. Our ancestors ordained, "An eye for an eye, and a tooth for a tooth," but I say unto you, you must not even oppose wrong to wrong. You must act to other people as you would wish them to act to you. If you have injured a man, it does not help you to be sorry for it if he hurts you back again. If you have done a wrong, it does not make you haste to repair it if men do another wrong to you. I say unto you that wrong can never be appeased by wrong. It can be swallowed up and blotted out by kindness only. Therefore, you must be gentle to those who are cruel to you, you must be merciful, you must not show contempt, you must not judge. You must forgive and be generous. And you must never despair, but go on being kind to all men, looking for no reward. These are the laws of the Kingdom of God.[2]

Impractical? On the contrary, such words are grounded in the deepest realism. "You must never despair, but go on being kind to all men, looking for no reward." Almost the complete antithesis of the usual standards of success, such a directive points the way to the illumination of life with a steady flame of hope.

2. "He died to make us good"

The reader will doubtless recognize these words as quoted, not from the Bible, but from one of the most familiar hymns of our Lord's suffering and death:

> He died that we might be forgiven,
> He died to make us good,
> That we might go at last to heav'n,
> Saved by His precious blood.[3]

There is a sense in which the death of a good and great man, especially if it is an unjust and violent death, not only shocks and saddens but inspires and lifts us. The deaths of Socrates and Lincoln, and nearer to our own time the deaths of Mahatma Gandhi and John F. Kennedy, have had this effect.

---

[2] (Garden City, N. Y.: Doubleday, Doran & Company, 1919), pp. 60-61.
[3] Cecil F. Alexander, "There is a green hill far away."

America is a purer nation for its unity in grief over the senseless murder of its late beloved though often unappreciated president, and the glowing words of his inaugural address will doubtless be remembered and quoted for years to come. Wherever this occurs and the man is remembered with admiration and love, as has been the case with Lincoln's unpretentious greatness for the past hundred years, human life will be lifted.

Yet this is by no means to say that the death of Jesus was simply that of a martyr to human misunderstanding. "So persecuted they the prophets"—before and since. But Jesus was more than a prophet. He was the Son of God; and the incarnation, the cross, and the resurrection are inextricably bound together.

The cross is not only by long tradition but by common agreement the central symbol of the Christian faith. This is because it stands at the focus of what God has done, is doing, and will do to the end of time for our salvation.

The death of Jesus cannot be rightly viewed as an isolated event. It has a before and after. The sweep of events, God's "mighty acts," of which this stands as the center may be taken as extending from the creation of the world to its final end, or from the making of the covenant with Israel to an expected second coming, or from the conception and birth of Jesus to his resurrection and the birth of the church. Whatever the scope of "holy history," the cross stands at its center. But not alone.

It is essential that the death of Jesus should be viewed in conjunction with his life. The incarnation, if it is to be seen as a real coming of God into human life, must be viewed in the context of history. Otherwise it becomes a theological abstraction. Thus, we need not hesitate to say that there were social, ecclesiastical, and political forces involved in Jesus' judicial murder. The crowd were fickle, and apparently disappointed when he turned out not to be the political Messiah—the son of David who would deliver them from the power of Rome and restore the nation to its former greatness. The Pharisees were angry at his disclosure of the barrenness of their boasted righteousness. The Sadducees wanted to keep their vested interests by standing in with the Roman government, and they saw in Jesus a disturbing influence. Back of all this Jewish opposition stood the Roman state, eager above all else to keep the peace by preserving the *status quo*, at least dimly aware that here was a new kind of principle that might prove a rival power.

Yet to stop at this point would equate the death of Jesus with the martyrdom of other good and great men, including those to whom reference has been made. The death of Jesus on the cross has had a strange power to redeem men from sin and hopelessness because it was the death of no ordinary man, but of the Son of God. To this unique fact both the wisdom of the Gospel writers and the deep intuitions of his followers through the centuries have borne witness. The New Testament rarely refers to Jesus as God; it calls him the Son of God. This is the more appropriate in view of his own obedience to and dependence on God the Father. But with great unanimity in spite of differences of understanding, his death has drawn men toward God because in it God himself was acting for our salvation.

This did not begin to happen at the hour of death, as some theories of the atonement might lead one to assume. God was in Christ throughout his ministry. We are told in a vivid word picture so characteristic of the Gospels that "Jesus went about all the cities and villages, teaching in their synagogues and preaching the gospel of the kingdom, and healing every disease and every infirmity" (Matt. 9:35). And this he did because he had a divine compassion for the people and felt a divine mission to bring them healing of body and spirit through the goodness and power of the Father.

We cannot understand with any realism the sacrificial dying of Jesus Christ for us and for all men unless through the pages of the Gospel record we can also catch glimpses of his sacrificial living. If we can enter into the story enough to see ourselves among those to whom he ministered—sinners forgiven, sick souls healed, despairing spirits lifted, self-centered lives turned outward, lives torn apart by the demons of unrest made whole again —then the simple but mysterious words, "He died for us," take on potency and profound meaning.

Not only must we view the death of Jesus in relation to what came before it, but what came after. We shall presently be speaking of the resurrection. But beyond the resurrection came the birth of the church, and the witnessing "in the power of the resurrection, and the fellowship of his sufferings," and the spread of Christianity around the world for the softening and strengthening of individual lives and great social groups. There is no realistic explanation of these fruits unless there was more in the living and dying of Jesus than in the life and death of a great, good man.

In this perspective it becomes easier to glimpse something of the eternal meaning of the cross. We cannot expect fully to rationalize it, for in it are compressed the mystery and miracle of God's saving love. Instead of trying to make it seem wholly reasonable, we had better say with Paul, "Thanks be to God for his inexpressible gift!" (II Cor. 9:15.) Yet the heart of its meaning is clear. It is the self-giving of God in suffering love for our salvation. It is God's way of reconciling men to himself and to one another, bridging the rifts of sin and establishing a new, a creative, and a joyous relationship. It is God's way of taking self-sacrifice, even to the utter self-giving of the best and purest of men, and making it the means by which others may come to triumphant living. In it the victim becomes the victor; the tragedy of Good Friday is turned to the triumph of the Easter morning.

The meaning of the cross is epitomized in Paul's words which suggest the deep convergence of who Jesus was, how he lived, how he died, and the difference it all makes. It has never been better stated, and it is doubtful that it could be. "God was in Christ reconciling the world to himself, not counting their trespasses against them, and entrusting to us the message of reconciliation." (II Cor. 5:19.)

Taken seriously, the message of the cross could not fail to make its impact on today's restless, despairing, largely self-centered, pleasure-engrossed world. Though we continue to adorn our churches with it, it stands as the antithesis of much that seems important in contemporary life. Beneath the veneer of superficial living the human heart cries out for what it offers, though what it demands in obedient love is less often recognized.

"He died to make us good"—with a goodness that goes deeper and rises higher than conventional morality. It is the goodness that comes with the motive-transforming, life-quickening good news of salvation through God's love. Where it has not been washed out through amalgamation with a semi-Christian culture —and even when, within the "suburban captivity of the churches," it breaks through the encasement of preoccupation with a multitude of competing claims—it comes with such power that life is made over and new hope is born.

3. "He is risen!"

Good Friday is not the last word. If it were, it would still be shrouded in darkness. Beyond it lies the resurrection morning.

To the followers of Jesus on that fateful spring day in Jerusalem the first Good Friday must not have seemed very good. The twelve had had a memorable evening with him the night before. In closest fellowship he had told them that he must leave them, had bidden them to keep his commandments by loving one another, had prayed that they and those who were henceforth to believe in him might all be one, had committed them to the care of the Father.

Apparently the whole situation was beyond the grasp of even our Lord's closest friends, for in his hour of agony they went to sleep, and when he was seized in the garden they all forsook him and fled. On the day of his crucifixion they must have had troubled spirits, and quite possibly some smitings of conscience.

And what of their own future? Their leader was dead. One reads between the lines the poignant despair in the words of the two who journeyed to Emmaus: "We had hoped that he was the one to redeem Israel" (Luke 24:21).

But something had happened! Over my desk hangs a picture of the sculptor Gutzon Borglum's "Mary Magdalene." The light of glad expectancy and renewed hope is in her eyes as she turns from the empty tomb to confront the living Christ. In one word, "Rabboni!" are compressed her gratitude, enduring devotion, joy. Gladness had replaced grief, and hope had been born.

So it was with the other followers of Jesus when this great news was known. Again and again he appeared to them until even the skeptical Thomas could no longer doubt. The little company came alive with news about which they could not be silent. God had conquered sin and death and had called them to witness to their faith in Jesus Christ. It was in this transforming resurrection experience that the Christian church was born.

The little company of Christ's followers grew—first from 12

to 120, then on Pentecost, when the Holy Spirit came upon them in power, to 3,000. Within our own time this movement has encircled the globe, for we are today the inheritors of that same victorious and hope-filled faith which no persecution or pain could daunt.

We do not know exactly what happened in the resurrection. The story is told in all four of the Gospels, and there are numerous references to it throughout the other books of the New Testament. Both because of this unanimity of witness and because of the transformation that came over the disciples with its ensuing effects, it is certain that it *did* happen. Attempts to explain it as a mythological account of a solely subjective, inner experience seem to me to require greater credulity than the Gospel narratives, which in spite of variations all read as if the occurrence were an objective one. These narratives have about them a note of mystery, as if the writers were trying to describe what is beyond human description. Yet they have about them also a note of great reality that certainly gave grounds for an assured faith and hope among the first Christians, and that still lifts our hearts with joy and hope on Easter morning.

Though I can claim no special wisdom in the matter, it does not seem to me that we are committed to either of the alternatives that the resurrection was solely an inner spiritual experience in the minds and hearts of the disciples or, on the other hand, that the same physical body with which Jesus died emerged from the tomb to pass through closed doors and eventually to ascend into the sky through a cloud. The one view affronts the pragmatic evidence, the other runs counter to all that we know of physiology and cosmology. In reference to our own eternal life we spoke, following Paul, of a "spiritual body," a vehicle of existence and communication which God will give us beyond death, but the nature of which we cannot know. May it not be that in the case of this unique Son of God, such a manifestation was granted to the disciples as an indisputable witness to the triumph of God over sin and death? In any case, the cross and the resurrection belong together as inseparable elements in our faith.

In the previous chapter the immortality or the resurrection of the individual human person was the main subject of consideration. Though care was taken to affirm that such eternal life is the gift of God, it must now be added that our fullest assurance of it stems from the resurrection of Jesus. "Because I live, you will live also" are words that never grow cold.

Here we must be careful not to make a misstep. The fact that Jesus Christ rose from the dead does not of itself guarantee our own resurrection. He was the divine-human Son of God; we are at best all too human sons and daughters of the Most High. None of us can expect to be present on earth after death in such a vivid and convincing form as the record tells us that he was. To assume that we shall be, or to expect it of our loved ones, tends toward ghostliness, not Christian hope. There *may* be such a thing as spirit communication in other ways, but we had better move guardedly at this point.

It is appropriate that the message of eternal life for the individual should be so often sounded on Easter morning. But not on the basis of any exact parallel with what happened in Jerusalem so many Easters ago. Rather, the heart of it lies in the goodness and power of God to bring triumph out of the deepest tragedy, life out of death, hope out of defeat and despair. The same goodness and power of God will give us what it is right for us to have, and by faith we may believe that this gift is eternal life, now and forever.

The author of the Epistle to the Hebrews glimpsed this connection perfectly in the benediction with which he closed his letter. It is no accident that we still use it as a benediction.

Now may the God of peace who brought again from the dead our Lord Jesus, the great shepherd of the sheep, by the blood of the eternal covenant, equip you with everything good that you may do his will, working in you that which is pleasing in his sight, through Jesus Christ; to whom be glory for ever and ever. Amen. (Heb. 13:20-21.)

4. "Lo, I am with you always"

According to Matthew's Gospel, the last words of Jesus to his disciples, following the great commission to go and make disciples of all nations, are the promise, "Lo, I am with you always, to the close of the age" (Matt. 28:20). Jesus' departure from the earthly scene as Luke describes it in the first chapter of Acts differs somewhat but with a great convergence beneath the surface. Here, too, is a commission with a promise. "But you shall receive power when the Holy Spirit has come upon you; and you shall be my witnesses in Jerusalem and in all Judea and Samaria and to the end of the earth." (Acts 1:8.)

The convergence in the mandate is clear enough, but what of the promise? In the one case it is the risen Christ who promises his continuing presence; in the other he promises power through the Holy Spirit. There is no conflict if we draw a natural conclusion; the living, present Christ *is* the Holy Spirit.

This is far more than a juggling of ideas to avoid contradiction. In the Old Testament there are numerous references to the Spirit of God, with the context indicating that the meaning is "God present" and "God acting." In the rare cases where the word "holy" precedes the term, as in the familiar prayer of Ps. 51:11,

> Cast me not away from thy presence,
> and take not thy holy Spirit from me,

"holy" is simply a descriptive adjective, to be written with a small "h."

In the New Testament, however, we find the Holy Spirit referred to not only as the Spirit of God but as the presence of the living Christ. It is significant that in the earliest New Testament writings, Paul's letters, he uses interchangeably and apparently with the same meaning the terms, "Holy Spirit," the "Spirit of God," the "Spirit of Jesus Christ," or simply "Christ," or the "Lord," or the "Spirit." The identification becomes complete in II Cor. 3:17, "Now the Lord is the Spirit."

This, to be sure, is not the only use of the term, for Jesus is said to have received the Holy Spirit at his baptism (Matt. 3:16; Mark 1:10; Luke 3:22; John 1:32), and on other occasions he or his followers are spoken of as "full of the Holy Spirit" or "led by the Spirit." In such instances the meaning seems to be a particular sense of the presence and power of God. Yet Paul's identification of the risen and living Christ with the Spirit of God was natural enough. It may well be followed by us, for it is our best index not only to an understanding of the Trinity but to an undergirding and vital sense of divine companionship.

As everpresent Companion—present, that is, to whoever will open the door to let him in—Jesus Christ is still the world's best hope. This is true whether we speak of the sinful, the distraught, the grief-stricken, or simply the shallow and empty lives of individuals, or of the giant evils that infest our society.

I have not said much in this volume about war, or communism, or nationalism, or racism, or materialism in its various forms. These issues have been discussed at some length in earlier books, and I feel deeply their seriousness.[4] But with all the complex

---

[4] Especially in *The Modern Rival of Christian Faith* (Nashville: Abingdon Press, 1952); and *Christian Ethics* (Nashville: Abingdon Press, 1957.)

problems in these fields which require the best political, economic, and civic wisdom—and for this no form of religious faith is a substitute—we must have also the wisdom, the power, and the presence of the God who was in Christ reconciling the world to himself. To us he has entrusted the message of reconciliation. If we Christians fail to witness to it and to let our acting be guided and empowered by it, the outlook is dark, for it is later than we tend to think.

There is much in the book of Revelation which is cryptic. Yet in the third chapter there is a description of the church in Laodicea which is crystal clear, bluntly and even inelegantly so:

> I know your works: you are neither cold nor hot. Would that you were cold or hot! So, because you are lukewarm, and neither cold nor hot, I will spew you out of my mouth. For you say, I am rich, I have prospered, and I need nothing; not knowing that you are wretched, pitiable, poor, blind, and naked (vss. 15-17).

Such words may seem a strange note on which to end a book on Christian hope—more appropriate, perhaps to a diatribe on our lukewarm churches or our even more tepid though supposedly Christian culture. Yet before the end of the paragraph are other words which epitomize our Christian hope. After a call to repentance, searching to the depths but not impossible of fulfillment, stands the promise: "Behold, I stand at the door and knock; if any one hears my voice and opens the door, I will come in to him and eat with him, and he with me. . . . He who has an ear, let him hear what the Spirit says to the churches" (vss. 20, 22).

The Spirit still speaks to the churches, both in reproof and in promise. Upon our response depends all that matters most.

INDEX